7/14

HACKNEY LIBRARY SERVICES

Please return this book to any library in Hackney, on or
before the last date stamped. Fines may be charged if it is late.
Avoid fines by renewing the book (subject to it NOT being reserved).

Call the renewals line on 020 8356 2539

People who are over 60, under 18 or registered disabled
are not charged fines.

⊕Hackney

PJ42014

LYRICAL FOUNTAIN

James Messam

To order additional copies of this book, contact:
Xlibris LLC
0-800-056-3182
www.xlibrispublishing.co.uk
Orders@xlibrispublishing.co.uk
523882

CONTENTS

Lyrically Armed...11

Lyrical Fountain 12

A day's trod 13

Progressive Practices 14

My Words 15

What is life?...18

This is my life 20

I Am Leaving This Place 21

Ready to Explode 22

My Lyrics 24

Daring and Courageous...26

Space Slam..27

The Voice Bell 29

Irresistible 30

Love Potion 32

Positive Violence..34

Magnetic Aura 35

Lovely as the Flowers 37

I Stand Alone...38

Optical Receptacle 40

Prisoner of the Future..41

Rejection...42

Report from the Lighthouse Fellowship 45

European Belief System 47

Religion...48

Battered and Bruised 50

I Will Not Acquiesce...51

Managing Change..53

Ambition...54

Stealing...56

Honesty 57

Monologue of a Teenager 58

Colloquialism 60

No Meds 61

The Future 62

Back a Yard 63

To My Roots 65

Questions 67

Battle of Fallujah 68

Learning to Read 70

Exotic Jahmeckya 72

Courage 76

Responsibility 77

Taking a Stand 78

From the Investigator 79

Determination 80

MY STORIES—READ AND REMINISCE

Reminiscent of My School Days 83

Spitfire Incorporation 85

It's better to Live in the Country 86

A Day of Fishing 88

Destruction of Bobby's House 90

First Class Test 92

Visions of the Past 94

Tro-Tro Pow-Pow 96

The Day My Cap Was Taken 98

Myself as a Waiter 100

An Unfortunate Situation 102

My Recollections 103

Putus in England 105

An Encounter with Roland Pile 107

Mrs. D 109

Exciting Days in Rock River 111

Testimony at Church 113

Frozen in My Tracks 115

Glossary 117

INTRODUCTION

After much deliberation, introspection and perspiration, I have taken time out to bring you this work. It is with great pleasure that I engage with your minds to present this my second work of creative expressions entitled 'Lyrical Fountain'. These vibrations are authentic and will cascade on your sensory faculties like an avalanche with atomic velocity.

I was born in the cool hills of North Central Clarendon in a small district called Suttons, a plantation from where 400 slaves escaped in 1690 to join the Maroons. I grew up in Rock River with my Aunt Beryl Miller. From an early age, I had an interest in the 'Spoken Word' following in the footsteps of my mother Eugenie Carridice, a renowned storyteller. My community work with Youth Clubs, Four H Clubs, and Jamaica Agricultural Society prepared me to develop my leadership potential and confidence in expressing myself in speech and drama activities. It was a regular custom of ours to have community concerts where we would act plays, sing songs, and recite poems and Bible verses. It was while at Mico Teachers College in Kingston Jamaica in the late seventies that my literary prowess blossomed when I was a member of The Afro-Caribbean Cultural and Debating Society.

I have been a teacher, social worker, cultural ambassador, orator, parish councillor, and above all performance poet, master of ceremonies, and researcher. My first book of poetry is entitled 'The Essence A Book of Poetic Expression" was published in 2007 by Ashwood House Publishing. This book 'Lyrical Fountain' is a continuation of my creative work, and I have decided to include some of my short stories that depict my experiences growing in the hills of Clarendon, where I spent most of my life close to nature on the banks of the Rio Minho River and the forests of the surrounding area.

I have been residing in the UK for the past decade where I have been very active in the creative arts and cultural expression of the diaspora. Freedom is a must. Confidence in self is vital.

I am confident that the contents of my work will bring pleasure and enlightenment to my friends, relatives, colleagues, and whoever cares to have a good source of inspiration. Embellish these words in your hearts, souls, and minds and be blessed.

ONE GOD, ONE AIM, ONE DESTINY.

ACKNOWLEDGEMENTS

Give thanks and praises to the Almighty Creative power of the Cosmos, the Alpha and Omega, Father and Mother of Iration, The Power of the Trinity JAH RASTAFARI AND EMPRESS MENEN.

I would like to acknowledge the invaluable help and inspiration from my Empress Millicent who has endured my indulgence in my creative endeavor. All my colleagues at Bethnal Green Academy (BGA) and my brethren Natty Culture who have helped with the positive vibrations; all my friends and colleagues from the Institute of Education (IOE), London, who have supported my creative works. To all my children, Stacy Ann, Albert, Michael, James Jr. Lamoya, and Semaj; my grandchildren, Kimoya, David and Kascha, my friends and relatives who have inspired me to engage in my work by supporting me in the past and the present. I say a huge thank you.

Big shout out to all my Spoken Word colleagues from 'Best Kept Secret' Word for Word and Original Son of Man, Prince Baden Junior, Dellmay and Jeff from Brixton Arts, and Mr. Gee; Nuff Raspect.

ONE LOVE.

LYRICALLY ARMED

(Chorus)
I'm lyrically armed but not dangerous
Don't get nervous or delirious
I'm not joking, I'm serious
One day to come I'll be famous

My lyrics are potent and furious
They are more lethal than a bazooka
Much sharper than the 'Cutting Edge'
On IRIE FM, hosted by Mutabaruka

I'm a lyrical warrior, armed to the teeth
More deadly than the venom from a cobra
Ready to break down any barrier
I'm versatile, volatile, and full of vitality
Calculated to inspire attention and retention
To increase your concentration
So that you can be reconditioned
Psychoanalyzed to create understanding
(Chorus)
My main tools are numerous word forms,
Adjectives, adverbs, alliterations, assonances,
Rhymes, rhythms, repetitions, intonations
Enunciations, pronunciations, pronouns, pauses,
Metaphors, meteors, similes, tones, and semitones
Create accelerated learning and increase earning
Optimizing the learning community
Develop more participation and unity.

LYRICAL FOUNTAIN

My lyrics are like a fountain
Cascading from the highest mountain
Disseminating vital information to the nation
Poetry is my medicine to heal your soul
Tune in to my dispensary for all the remedies
From the escalating maladies of modern technologies
Deforestation, mass production, commercialization
Consumerism and gross exploitation
Of our natural resources increases global warming
Resulting in the melting of the ice caps and flooding

My poetic techniques are authentic not cosmetic
Humane, not static, constantly vibrating
Oscillating and captivating
Unlocking your latent thought processes
Inciting your sublime consciousness
Awakening your mental ability
To achieve its maximum capacity

Developing a vibrant vocabulary
Is primary not secondary or tertiary
Select and read from a variety of sources
Infuse these impulses in your nervous system
Let them vibrate on your cochlea
Echoing through your spinal chord
Disturbing the equilibrium of your cerebrum
Rocketing to your cranium making you feel
Electrifying, magnifying, and beautifying

A DAY'S TROD

Early in the morning I awake from my slumber
Preparing for a day of productive endeavour
Leaving home early in the misty dawn
Everything seems so calm
Trodding through Holdbrook Park
I see the lights as they flicker in the dark
Yellow and white shining so bright
It's such a beautiful sight

My ruddy cheeks caressed by the cool breeze
I hear the birds chirping in the overhanging trees
They sing melodious songs intermingled
With the incessant humming of traffic on the M25
I feel my system come alive
As I briskly walk to the bus terminus
Humming a little song as I trod along
Can't be weak, got to be strong
To face the day's activities
Anticipating exciting, engaging encounters

PROGRESSIVE PRACTICES

Teaching and learning are integral processes of life
Whether explicit or implicit we must give credence
To the articulation of relevant concepts
Embedded in the relevant discourses
As we undertake the immense journey
Of inculcating positive values and attitudes
Replicating tangible structured learning styles
Whatever the task to be undertaken
We must strive to do our best
Sometimes we cannot rest
We must endure and uphold our integrity

Though the future appears to be dim
We must be bold from without and within
Our fear we must put aside
We cannot run, we cannot hide
Every day is a new day, working hard and smart
Sometimes humming our favourite rhymes
Using established as well as unconventional techniques
To teach or learn new concepts that will be beneficial
To the group or individual
Whether musically or dramatically
We must work together in harmony.

MY WORDS

My words are my bond
My words make me strong
My words make me feel right
With my words I can put up a fight
My words are my possession
My words are like a prescription
When everything else fails
With my words I will prevail

My words are my inspiration
My desire, my great expectation
I speak my words with conviction
I make it clear my intention
Over, beneath, and beyond
My words are my bond
My words make me feel strong

When family and friends forsake
It's to my words I relate.
My words represent me
Shelter and protect me
My words make me feel sublime
Away with violence and crime
Why should we fuss and fight
When it's better for us to unite?

Brothers and sisters be strong,
Let your words be your bond
Whether you are male or female
Black or white, literate or illiterate
Your words tell who you are
You could be a superstar
Develop your vocabulary
Always consult your dictionary

Read and write stories of your social,
Cultural and political heritage
Be bold, for half the story
Has never been told
Of the confidence of the sages
Open your books turn the pages
Read and be wise, open your eyes
Embrace the positive contributions
The ultimate strength and determination
Constant challenges and confrontations
Personal sacrifices and deprivations

Refocus your energies and efforts
Build bridges to connect your soul
From which you have been detached
Explore avenues to bolster your knowledge
Strive for fulfillment and enlightenment
Recognized nurture and appreciate
Words as the most potent resources
Cultivate a wide and vibrant vocabulary
Tap into this unique quality of solace
In order to overcome obstacles

Words are powerful
Words are beautiful
Words can motivate and elucidate
Words can captivate and educate
Through words you can communicate
Words can ignite passion
Words can take you on a mission
Words can tear us apart
Words can mend a broken heart

Let's make a start and use words like
Peace, love, unity, opportunity
Stability and ability in the community
To inspire confidence, self-reliance
Self-determination, self-esteem
Self-awareness, self-actualization
To improve the life of our nation
My words are my bond
It's to my words that I belong
My words make me strong.

WHAT IS LIFE?

What is life you may ask?
That's the big question
Which deserves an honest answer?
For centuries humans have been perplexed
By this burning desire to decipher
The concept of this elusive idea of life;
Different civilizations have evolved
Developed, prospered, and disappeared
In the annals of our psychic
Yet we are nowhere nearer to solving
The mystery of the beginning of life

There has been such a wide diversity
Of perceptions and opinions advanced
Yet the mystery deepens with new revelations
For the more things and times change
The more they remain the same
Some say life is what you make it
Others say it's real you cannot fake it
Life is just for living, so live the life you love
Let love flow like a blessing from above

Is this some kind of weird game?
That is being played on the world stage
To get us all in a frantic frenzied rage?
Where one power is pitted against another
Sons against fathers, daughters against mothers
When did this all begin? When will it ever end?
You are not my enemy, just be my friend.

THIS IS MY LIFE

(Chorus)

This is my life; you can't take it away
I won't let go, no way, no way
I won't go astray, 'cause I'm here to stay
I'll hold on in every way

I will fight for my life, not giving up
Though I face trials and tribulations
I'll keep holding on, got to be strong
I will always do the right thing, day or night
The sun is shining, breeze is blowing
Early in the morning I'm doing my farming

(Cho)

When the pressures of life seem to hold you down
Wear a big smile and not a frown
Got to hold on, never let go
Jah love you so, that you must know
He will bear you up like the wings of an eagle
Take you to your desired haven
Giving you comfort when you feel despair
He is never far away, always near

(Cho)

I will not give up, must sip the cup
On my way down or on my way up
No matter the trials and tribulations
I will remain resolute and strong
No retreat no surrender
I will fight and not go under
My mind is made up
Climbing from the bottom to the top

(Cho)

I AM LEAVING THIS PLACE

I am leaving this place
It's just a big disgrace
The way they are treating me
Are you blind? Can't you see?
That the cards are stacked
We are under attack
Yet we dare not fight back

Can't take this crap
Got to make it stop, stop brap
My heart is pounding faster in my chest
Night and day I cannot rest
I am burning with desire
Like a raging fire on a barbed wire
Raising my temperature higher and higher
Must return to the Island of my birth
My fortune lies in tilling the earth
Establishing orchard crops for posterity
Reconnecting to my roots for stability
These concrete castles only entrap my body
But my soul is free to establish contact
With my future sustenance not just pittance
With this in mind I can sing and dance.

READY TO EXPLODE

My mind is like a dam waiting to explode
And deliver its heavy load
With catastrophic consequences
Stripped of my language and culture
They devour my spirit like a vulture
Erasing memories of scenes
Etched on my fertile mind
I search but cannot find
The path to my very existence
I will intensify my resistance
To this parasitic system
Seeking to keep me subservient
Must manifest my reverence
To the Alpha and the Omega
Mother and Father of creation
Beginning and end of time

From the recesses of my eclectic mind
Replete with a unique array of extraordinary
Fascinating, daunting, diverse illustrations
Transcending time and space to penetrate
A captivating concentration of energy
Emanating from the depth of my consciousness
A diverse concoction of cosmic radiation
Exploding like a volcanic fountain
Invigorating the vegetation as it descends
To the outermost regions of the mountainside
Bringing moisture to the once parched pasture

As I stand motionless in my meditation
Visions of the past flicker on my nervous system
Evoking a feeling of awakening from my slumber
Enlivening my subconscious to an alertness
Penetrating the labyrinth of my prolific
Functional, fruitful, fearless frontier
My conviction is undaunted in a peculiar
Evolutionary, enveloping, enthralling encounter
An intricately interwoven diversity, deserving attention
Combining relevant information for dissemination
In all teaching and learning institutions

MY LYRICS

(Chorus)

I spit my lyrics in time
To speak my mind is not a crime.

Really hope you are fine
Look at me, can't you see?
It's not fantasy but reality,
Crime and violence in the community
The shooting and stabbing on the street
Complain from people that you meet

(Chorus)

Why? Why? Is the constant cry?
Do our youths have to die?
What is the cause of this?
Is there something gone amiss?
What can we do to remedy this situation?
That is wreaking havoc to the nation?
Why are the youths so cold?
To the young and the old?

(Chorus)

Sometimes I sit and wonder
Why our youth have to die
Why should we destroy each other?
Aren't we sisters and brothers
Aunts, uncles, nieces, nephews,
Fathers and mothers

What has gone wrong?
Why are we so weak?
When we should be strong
Is it lack of love and devotion?
Or just careless destruction?

(Chorus)

DARING AND COURAGEOUS

Courage is a very strong element of living
Without courage we would only exist
This is a basic survival instinct
Inherent in even micro cellular specimens
As humans we must exude courage
Bolstered in confidence that we will soar to the top
And not wither at the base of human depravity.

We can draw strength from our fore parents
Who have stood up against all the odds
To achieve our liberation
It is our duty to be bold
Daring and courageous
To retain the semblance of liberty
That we take for granted.

'Up you mighty Race
You can accomplish what you will'
So says Marcus Mosiah Garvey.
'Leadership means everything.
Pain, suffering, sacrifice, and even death'
A people without knowledge of their History
Is like a Tree without roots
That cannot stand but wither away
Yes! Ah so Mr. Marcus say.

SPACE SLAM

Bang! Bang! Bang!
This is the bang
The big, big bang
Where it all began
Space is big, big, big, and big
Vastly, hugely, mind bogglingly big

Our universe is on the move;
Get in the grove
Millions of galaxies
Are spiraling on the milky—way
At galactic speed, extending into infinity
Outside the realms of reality
Defying the forces of gravity

The search is on, has been going on
From time immoral
Technological advances, circumnavigation,
Shifted vast populations
From the African continent
To the Americas bringing genocide
To the indigenous inhabitants
Due to greed and gross violations
Imperial expansion, Industrialization,
Innate feelings of superiority

In the past, present, and future
Meteorites escaped from space
Bringing valuable information
About the Solar system
As Astrologers, Astronomers, Archaeologist,
Geologists and Physicists seek valuable solutions
To societies myriads of problems

The Astrolabe; a scientific instrument predates
Clocks, telescopes, and stethoscopes,
Star map helps to define religion,
Time keeping and navigation of the vast oceans
Tick, tock, clickety clock, declination to ascension
Cosmic microwave background produces black holes
This can absorb matter, scatter, and flatter litter
Whether you are an Earthling or Space ling
Just tune into my slam.

THE VOICE BELL

The Voice Bell is unique
Creative and integrated
It lets you leave a clue
To get back to you
It doubles as a Voice Mail Service
For messages even when you are not there

It has a competitive advantage
Uniquely positioned with a cutting edge
Creating a persistent consistent approach
Setting a goal to be focused on as
A passionate, affectionate, and effective idea
This can withstand the test of time
To make your life sublime

The Voice Bell lets you leave a clue
To get back to you
It's simple; yet communicative
Don't fret or worry your cognitive
Just press the buzzer and speak
To leave your message
It's easily available retail or wholesale
Affordable, dependable, and indispensable

IRRESISTIBLE

You are irresistible, desirable, fascinating,
Genuine, sincere, and constantly captivating
Your iridescent presence illuminates
The surroundings, compelling rapt attention
As we gaze with fascination
At your alluring countenance
That glows with intensity
Magnetizing the atmosphere
With great density,
Capturing the entire vicinity
Enthralling the community
With awe and inspiration
To be enveloped in your illustrious
Salubrious, sumptuous, harmonious,
Gracious and attractive splendor

You are my desire, my great expectation,
My beautiful flower; let us get together
Remain forever, like birds of a feather
My heart beats faster and faster
When you light my fire
Taking me higher and higher
Soaring like a tower
Hold me in your arms
Let me experience your charms
Bubbling like a fountain twirling
Surging to the captivating
Rhythm of life as we heave
Gyrating, expressing our desire
Our deep fascination to an
Irresistible pulsating sensation
On this wonderful occasion
Love is the only solution.

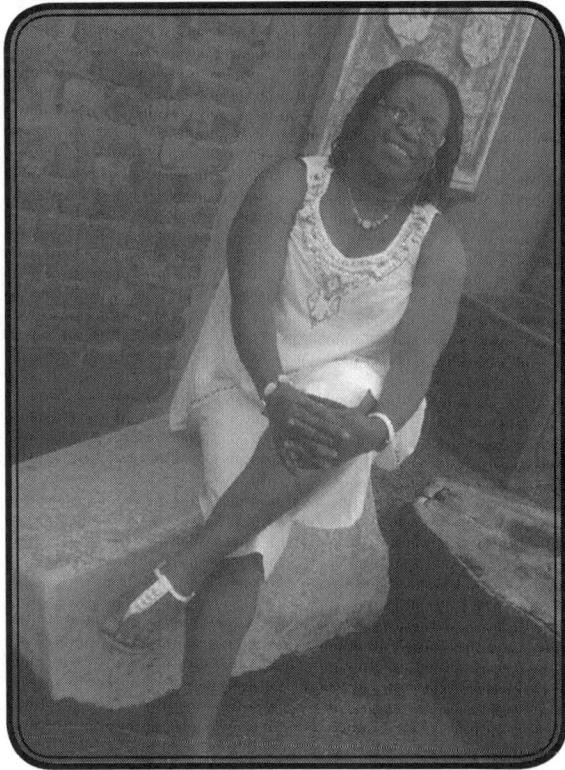

LOVE POTION

I admire your beautiful countenance
Your sturdy neck and firm physique
Your unhurried gait gliding like a gazelle
So bold exhibiting no fear as your ebony locks
Reach you shoulder making you look bolder
Your ebony white teeth glisten
In the exuberant sunshine

I like to embrace your curvaceous body
And caress your cheeks, look in your eyes
As they sparkle with glee
On account of my close proximity
My beloved I desire thee
I am yours and you are mine for eternity

Oh! How I love you so much
Longing for your tender touch
A massive adrenalin rush
Making me really blush
Want to caress your star apple breast
As you rub down the hair on my chest
Night and day I cannot rest
To me you are the very best

In the stillness of the night
When everything is quiet
We slip away together
Like birds of a feather
Arm in arm strolling along
Singing a melodious song
Minds attuned to the wonders of nature
Looking forward to a peaceful future

Trodding along with an unhurried gait
Never too soon, never too late
Working for a brighter future
For our sisters and brothers
Mothers and fathers
For everyone in the world
Man, woman, boy, or girl

Sitting by the riverside watching the tide
Having you by my side
I reach out to touch your face
And give you a warm embrace
Come along and sing this song
As the cool water flows along
Hear the birds chirping in the trees
Blowing to and fro from the cool breeze

POSITIVE VIOLENCE

Kill me softly with your love
Slay me tenderly with your concern
Suffocate me passionately with your hug
Knock me mercilessly to the ground with kindness
Devastate my emotions with your tone of voice
Massacre my senses brutally with your stare

Tear my heart apart with your goodbye
Bring me to tears by telling me that you are leaving
Give me a goodbye kiss, something I will surely miss
Let your tears caress my cheeks like a waterfall.
Drown me with your weeping eyes
Hold me tight like you will never let me go

Procrastinate your departure indefinitely
Tell me you have nowhere else to go
Squeeze me passionately close to your torso
Until my temperature reaches boiling point
Scratch my aching back until it sizzles with pain
I will stand at attention in the pouring rain
Endure the striking lightning and the pealing thunder

My darling love, leave me not asunder
I've realized that I have made a blunder
I will compensate and restore tenfold
Even to the extent of depleting my billfold
My whole life is engulfed in your happiness
Let's stay connected and be blessed

MAGNETIC AURA

Your magnetic aura evokes feelings of great desire
Melting in your arms; mystified,
Enthralled and spellbound
The tender touch of your arms around my torso
Sends my mind in a tailspin,
A hazy feeling of melancholy happiness
An exuberant feeling as we kiss and caress

Bedazzled by your humility, your eloquent expression
Floating elegantly on my auditory canal
Inhaling the fresh fragrance of the morning air
Attracted by a sizzling sensation
An incredible, sensitive, and tantalizing ardour
A saturated, coordinated feeling floating in the air
Marinating on my mental hemisphere
Your infectious glorious sunshine like smile
Creates an incredible, irresistible, desirable feeling

Your pleasant countenance and petite physique
Arouses erotic fantasies, igniting with great intensity
My mental faculty is enlivened and sparkles with luminance
Spreading through my entire being
My optical receptacle captures images of your pleasant features
My fingers wander gently on your velvet like skin
As you slither closer to my torso
Entwined within my upper and lower extremities
My heart palpitates at an accelerated pace
As the moist breath exhale from your nostrils

The curvature of your slender body fully enveloped in my grasp
As my adventurous tongue probes the curvature of your breast
I feel your body heave in an upward trust
Creating a sudden emotional rush
Enlivening my estuary, creating a feeling of bliss
With great intensity as the friction ignites in passion
As I gentle penetrate your moist central hemisphere

LOVELY AS THE FLOWERS

You can be as lovely as the flowers
Each second, each minute each hour
Just be natural, real, and heartical
Unadulterated not artificial
Spontaneous like a spark of flame
Leaping forward to its domain
Unfettered like the sun that shines
Darling you are surely mine

It would be a joy to be lovely
As a flower in your sight
Your smile, hugs, and kisses
Can enhance and nurture the flower
As it blooms profusely
Sharing is wonderful and truly lovely
I love you endlessly
I will endeavor to do my best
To bring out the essence of your been
If you fathom what I mean
Be patient and strong to ensure
Togetherness of spirit and soul
Our love will endure whatever vicissitudes
That may emerge on our journey
As we travel through time and space
Remember we are specimens of the human race
No doubts or inhibitions just love and devotion.

I STAND ALONE

I stand alone
Far away from home
Forlorn like a dove
Searching to find the one I love
I yearn for your company
As I sit on this balcony
Alone to myself,
Far away from anyone else

I long for your touch
Oh! I miss you so much
The soft sound of your voice
Your tender touch was so nice
I miss your warm embrace,
The pleasant smile on your face
I'm alone to myself,
Far away from anyone else

I looked all around for you
I searched but didn't find a clue
To the happiness that I seek
As I trod along on my feet
But there was no one to meet
As I searched the desolate street
I'm alone to myself,
Far away from anyone else

I remember the times we spent together
We were so happy with each other
Enjoying the pleasures of life
Free from stress or strife
Circumstances tore us apart
Oh! How it broke my heart
Now I'm alone to myself,
Far away from anyone else

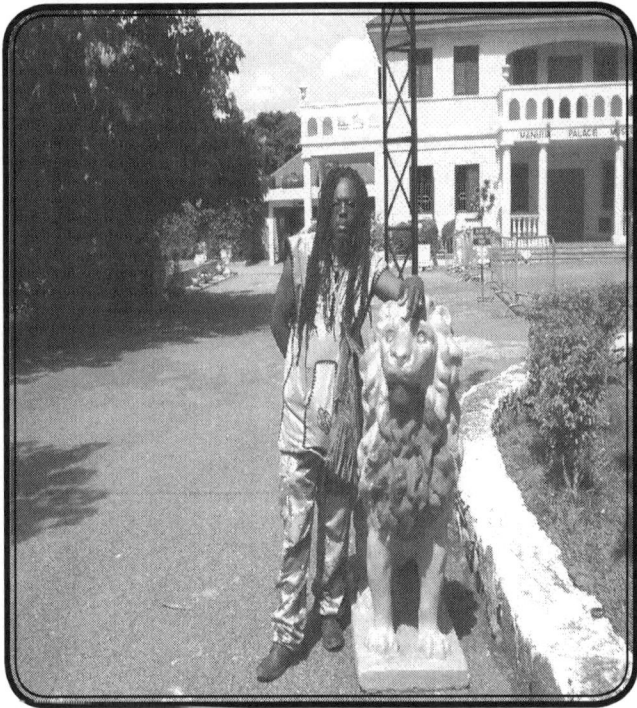

OPTICAL RECEPTACLE

As I focus my optical receptacle in your direction
A clear illustration caught my imagination
I gazed and gazed with rapt attention
At the image that caught my fascination
Realising we were bound for the same destination
Looking at that beautiful smile
That seems to stretch for a thousand miles
My mind went into overdrive
As I was propelled to come alive
As those deep blue eyes sparkle with glee
Beloved I desire thee
To be my pavilion in which I can hide
As we go riding in that boat by the riverside.

Say what! You are not lonely?
You do not desire my company?
We are not compatible?
Oh! You are so wrong.
Come along; let me hold your hand
And take you to the 'Promised Land'
Where the verdant pastures grow
There is exuberant sunshine, no snow
The lush green vegetation
Is our only habitation
Birds sing sweetly in the trees
Fishes swim gracefully in the seas
The fisherman strolls leisurely on the sand
Come darling; let me take your hand

PRISONER OF THE FUTURE

My heart is a prisoner of the future
I yearn to venture in the labyrinth of your soul
To bask in the glory far untold
My arms ache to hold you my dear
Be brave, have no fear
You can enslave my body but not my soul
For my soul dwells in the house of tomorrow
Which you cannot enter not even in your dreams

You can deny my existence
But you cannot obliterate my Essence
It's the ether of my being
I care not who you are
Or what they say about you
I crave your undivided affection
Your unfettered attention
Your incessant desire for a feel of my fire
Burning within the splendor of your cardiac center
Where only the pure can enter

As I reach out to engulf you in my sturdy arms
Where you can experience my tender charms
In every heart, every soul, every mind
Many have died because of neglect
Give thanks and praises to the Almighty
The Power of the Trinity
When all else fails He will surely prevail.

REJECTION

Actions speak loudly,
Even the blind can see
The way you are treating me
Why must you treat me like this?
Is there something gone amiss?
You do not respond to my touch
Yet you declare that you love me so much
You never have time for me, a total stranger
Our relationship is in danger
You resent my facial hair,
Even the clothes I wear

Sometimes I stand and stare
To ascertain if you are aware
Of the pain and suffering
That you perpetuate
You said, you love me
But I am not sure anymore
You have never treated me like this before
Is there something you are not telling me?
Or I'm too damn blind to see?

I refuse to surrender
To your whims and fancies
Your selfish desires and motives
I'd rather leave than remain
In this subservient situation
I have my pride and ambition,
My dreams and aspirations
I'm not suffering in silence;
I will not resort to violence
My mind is made up;
I've had enough of this rejection
Therefore I quit!

Say what!
You don't understand
What kind of man I am
Walking out of a good relationship
Take that back—
This ship is sinking!
It's drifting dangerously,
Descending in an abyss
There is no satisfaction
Without some affection
All I get is neglect,
Humiliation and dejection
Constant, frequent, incessant rejection

You are always tired;
Never have time for my advances
Turning your back,
Making all sorts of excuses
Nothing in life last forever,
Whatever, whenever; never
We said, 'Till death do us part,
For better or for worse'
I'd rather go asunder than surrender
It's time to move on and get myself together
No need for goodbye or feelings of remorse
For it's better to be a Bushman
Than be subservient in your Palace

I'm leaving this sinking ship,
This lopsided unfulfilled relationship
This so-called Palace,
All I get is rejection and malice
There is a gulf between us,
Living in a parallel world
Before my eyes the truth unfold
From my Hell I see you in your Heaven
All decked in our make belief
Exhibiting an air of arrogance

Living in a world of fear
Hiding under a veil of pretense
We cannot get under this fence
Neither can we get around
Beyond, beneath, above, or over

This gulf separates us,
One from the other
Our mental, emotional,
Physical, spiritual, and
Psychological faculties
Are not on the same frequency
We cannot communicate,
We can only remonstrate.
There is no response to the impulses
Emitting from our transformers
Our antennas are not cued
They are out of sync
Rendering communication impossible, obsolete
Dysfunction, irrational, illogical, nonsensical
No harmony, in fact—**total black out**

I'm frustrated and furious,
Your excuses are too numerous
Every day it is getting more dangerous
More hazardous, perilous, and cantankerous
Can't you see what this is doing to me?
Or are you too blind to see?
Or you just don't care as you stand and stare
At my rugged Natty Congo Hair
Living in fear of your denial
Or is this your way of being Genial?

REPORT FROM THE LIGHTHOUSE FELLOWSHIP

Dear Brother Paul; one and all
Thanks for your invitation
To this special occasion and location
For the Light House Fellowship celebration
At the Battersea Arts Centre Lavender Hill
I was not early just a little late
This is a story I have to relate

In this age of 'Enlightenment'
And technological advancement
Proliferation of ideas and religious propagation
It was to my utter consternation and total trepidation
Coupled with gross disbelief after great anticipation
Of sharing my poetic inspiration with the congregation
That low and behold I was told that I was not allowed
To make my contribution due to my Rastafarian persuasion

The event was billed as a 'Friends and Family Day'
But I am sad to say that it was a day of discrimination
Mass violation and total lack of toleration
The promised prosperity and wonderful peace
Healthy and humane consideration to the congregation
Was but a fleeting illusion to be pursued but never attained.
As you prophesied in Jesus's name
Yet your actions remain the same

It's all a pretense dressed in your 'Sunday best'
With no care or concern for the basic concept
Like peace, love, and equality in the society
You quote from different passages
Delivering your so-called messages
To the unlearned and gullible
Reading from your Authorised Bible
It's time that you stop and think
You are heading for the brink
Of no return, sinking in a quagmire
Surely you will burn in hot fire.

EUROPEAN BELIEF SYSTEM

The European belief system
Stagnates the growth and development
Of the African spiritual fulfillment
His dreams and aspirations
A tonnage of guilt and sin has
Weighted down his consciousness
His mind is warped by a belief system
That has been imposed on his mental,
Physical, psychological orientation
This has stagnated and poisoned
His ability to think outside the 'Box'

He has been programmed to leave everything to Jesus
Where the Black mans' God? His Alpha and Omega
Why, why must he deny the very existence of himself?
His features, his language and culture
He has become a vulture,
A cannibal, eating the carcass of animals
Blackman arise and take control of your own destiny
Liberate your minds from your oppressors' belief system

The Blackman knew God for centuries before the Europeans
You will always be a slave if you are stuck in their belief system
Their 'Psycho Visora' personal scruples, mental desires
Religions have created the most destructive events in history
For too long you have been a slave from the womb to the tomb
Free yourself from mental shackles
The yoke of oppression and destitution
'The European belief system'

RELIGION

Different religions purport that
Their god is the only God.
It is wrong and biased for
Us to disregard other people
Because they do not accept our belief
Everyone must account for his/her own actions
We should not condemn other people
If they do not share our belief
We are all entitled to our own way of life.
Grown up with a Christian background
I find it very uncomfortable when
Christians say their way of life is the only way.
It is written that Christ says that the wheat and tears
Should be allowed to grow together
To await the day of harvest
I consider it very limiting for us to condemn
Others due to their religious belief
Karl Marx describes religion
As the 'opium of the poor'
In essence it is the poor and depressed
Filling up the pews in the numerous Churches,
Synagogues and Mosques all over the world
They have been inculcated to believe
That a great God will descend from the sky
Save them, make them happy and not die
They are seeking to go to 'Heaven'
A place that has been concocted
To lure them into complete obedience
To the whims and fancies of the so-called
Church of God whose son Jesus Christ
Died to save mankind from sin

The same concept that has entrapped us
Will not now prove to be our Saviour
Marcus Garvey says—
'No powerful people will give
Less powerful people the reins of power
Just because they ask for it'
We must be in a position to demand,
Command respect, unity and integrity

BATTERED AND BRUISED

Battered, bruised, and abused
Neglected, despised, shunted, and shifted
Stained, maimed, marginalized, and hung to dry
Given the cynical sneer, stare in full glare
To belittle my integrity, ruffle my countenance
Denigrate my persona into oblivion
I will not bow nor will I flinch an inch

Bitter, boiling, bleeding, minds swirling
Thoughts unfurling, feel like shouting—
Feel like shouting yet naught revealing
Heart is reeling: my skin is peeling
What is this that I'm feeling?
On my knees I'm kneeling
To the Almighty I'm pleading

Un-retreating, just advancing, chanting
Fly, fly, fly caged bird fly
Unfurl your wings and fly to the sky
This is the truth not a lie
Here but I didn't come from here
It was not of my own free will
I will not leave until I get a fair share
Of the pie in the sky

Why does it have to be like this?
Oh! How I wish I were in Paradise
In ambience of pastures fresh and green
Cane fields bow their heads to the gentle breeze
Bamboo and coconut trees sway to and fro
Succulent mango juice runs down my chin
Licked by my moist tongue
Oh! How I longed for that solace
That inward feeling of bliss
To live and love to my heart's desire
Free from fear and stress and be blessed.

I WILL NOT ACQUIESCE

You have trampled on my dignity
Crushed the last vestige of my self esteem
I'm seething with rage because of pain
You have even changed my name
But I will not acquiesce to your cruelty
Neither will I act with sheer brutality
For I must maintain my sanity
My essence as a specimen of humanity
Don't take my meekness for weakness
For I am more than able to address
The calamities that you instigate
Through your system of hate

Intimidation, provocation and deprivation
Brainwash education, false indoctrination
Attribution, theological conceptions
Compilation, commentaries and perspectives
Conspiracy, interpolation, incredible doxologies
Has been programmed in the psychic of the nation
Doctrines of lies and gross inerrancy for generations
Misconceptions in—genuine authenticity
Verbal plenary explanation of the Bible
To confuse and miss-inform the gullible
Your historians, so called prophets and soothsayers
Men of the pulpit lie and instigate falsehood
Every day on the television and other media
To infiltrate manipulate and perpetuate
'The Great Deception' from your Theologians

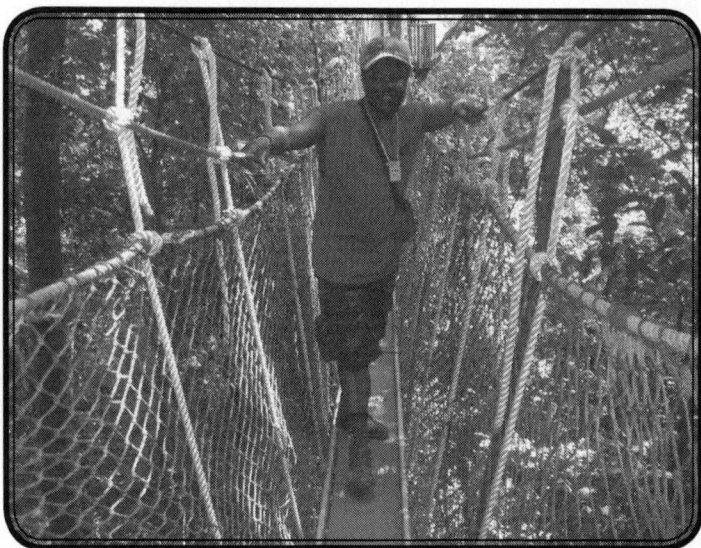
On the Canopy—Kakum National Park in Ghana (2007)

MANAGING CHANGE

Residents are the focal point of the community
They must be given a chance to make decisions
They must be engaged in the affairs of the state
The actions that matter to their daily living
Training is essential in order to prepare them to cope
And make management decisions, create partnerships
The relationship between the elected representatives
And the people must be taken into consideration
Change must be influenced responsibly
It should not be allowed to happen haphazardly
Change must be managed effectively
There is a revolution taking place all over the world

We must eke out an existence
From the scant resources at our disposal
Can't grumble or grunt
Must survive and stay alive,
Crime brings grime in our neighborhoods
Deprivation, sufferation, neglect, abject poverty
Creates unease, breathes disease
Pollution, drought, underachievement,
These make no sense, high unemployment,
People are judged as a result of their post code
Discriminated against due to stereotypical reputation
We must demand genuine regeneration,
More innovative methods of involvement
To generate improvement and uplift for the environment

AMBITION

What is your ambition?
What is your motivation?
Your source of inspiration
What goads you into action?
What is the reason for all these questions?
Does it have to do with your complexion?
Or I want to gauge your reaction?

What gives you satisfaction?
Is it addiction, compassion, or affection?
Rise to the occasion
Be of some value to your nation
Don't stand in consternation
Make it clear your intention
Make this your fervent declaration

Self-realization, active participation
Will generate a better solution
Throughout the population
Make it clear in your application
That you must have job satisfaction
To achieve your stated agitation
Why must you suffer such humiliation?

Stop and search is on the increase
Constant interrogation from the Police
Especially if you are from the 'Global Majority'
Or if you live in a certain locality
Victimization, discrimination, intimidation
Sufferation, alienation, and deprivation
Is the constant mode of operation
Education is the solution to
This entire negative situation

My loving daughters, Lamoya and Stacy Ann

STEALING

It is a sin to steal a pin, much more a bigger thing
Every liar is a thief, a very dangerous specimen
He or she will put others in problems
Causing suspicion and cynicism
Avoid such a person at any cost,
Shun him/her, keep them at bay
Never let them tarry in your vicinity

As they are dishonest, dishonourable, and of ill repute
Shun them, snob them as it is very embarrassing,
Distressing and very off putting, disconcerting
To have such a person in your company
They could smear your character
Casting aspersion on your integrity
This type of behavior will create dis-unity

Do not condone their presence
For with all the betwixt and between
Things are not necessarily how they seem
They will do and say things just to snare you
Open your eyes and ears constantly
Do not be fooled by their pretense of sincerity
It's just a charade for their impunity

Some people think that it is cool
To take things when no one is looking
But you should be your own master
Or your selfish action will lead to disaster
For whatever goes on in the darkest part
Will be revealed to break your heart
So practice honesty as the best policy
In your home, school and community

HONESTY

Your esteem is bolstered by
Truthfulness and self—awareness
Positive re-enforcement
Helps to develop insight and intuition
A good foundation is
Essential for self—determination
In order to experience the positive flow of energy
Making a difference in your life;
Even for a brief moment
Practice the essential skills of
Self-confidence and endurance
Coupled with conflict resolution in a sincere, conscious,
Consistent, considerate approach with a strong work ethic
And a desire to fulfill your dreams and aspirations

Rock the boat if you must but remember your goal
Endeavour to rise to the occasion with intelligence
Passion with strong motivation to explore and pursue
Your visual and auditory connections to stay attached
To your roots and culture which drive your growth
Remember your ancestors who have paved the way
Sacrificing their lives for you to have a brighter future
Sustain the struggle; strive for the prize that's afar
Seek and you will find whatever you are looking for.

MONOLOGUE OF A TEENAGER

The whole world is against me,
Just because I told my friend that I was gay.
My mum is nowhere around to support me
I'm having problems at school
Due to my sexual orientation
Nobody listens to me,
Even my teachers don't care.
I get bullied all the time

When I retaliate I get excluded from school.
Now I am at the Pupil Referral Unit
These guys introduce me to drugs
I make money shotting and it seems good
Dad warned me about the dangers involved.
He told me how my freedom
Could be taken away one day
I didn't listen to his advice.

Now I am locked up in a
Young Offenders Institution
I long for my home, and relatives,
Even my teachers and friends at school
Why didn't I listen and follow instructions?
Things could have been different, now I repent.

From the age of ten
I started to wear the veil.
It was not my choice.
My parents said, I had to wear it
My sisters have to wear it
As it was part of our tradition,
A part of our way of life
It's a burden we have to bear
What will my friends think?

Is it going to change my life?
At school my friends abandon me
They don't want to associate with me
I've been accused, convicted, and condemned.
They have been my accuser,
Judge, jury, and executioner
I was not given a chance to defend myself

My mind is in a state of confusion;
Very soon there will be an explosion.
My back is against the wall
My friends and families forsake me;
The contrived evidence points at me
My picture is on TV and in the newspapers
I am tortured, battered, and bruised.

They want me to confess.
What should I do? I didn't do it.
It makes no difference.
It's just me against the world.
Why do they look at me differently?
If I go out for a walk
The Police stop and search me
Just because I wear my prayer hat

The things I see on TV,
Hear on the radio or read in the newspapers,
Make me feel angry and distressed
These people have gone too far
Trying to destroy our Religion; our way of life
We must stand up for our rights;
To defend our dignity, we will fight
If necessary as we are confident
In the victory of good over evil

COLLOQUIALISM

Nuh badda worry, nuh badda fret
If yu nebba hear nutten like dem yah yet
Wha go up must cum dung
Dere must be a start before a finish
Nuh heng yu coat whey yu can't reach it
When yu a dig pit, dig two
If yu spit inna de sky, it aggo fall inna yu yeye'
Cut yu coat according to yu clath
Ah nuh same day leaf drap inna wata it ratten
Nuh dash whey yu tick till yu crass de riva
De higher de monkey climb ah de more him expose
De bigga de fish de more oil it teck fi fry
De fax can't get de grape him sey it sowa
When yu han inna lion mouth
Teck time draw it out
Big fish wag him tail any whey
If pus an dawg ah n'nam outta di same plate
Ah fi pus de food
Duppy know who fi frighten
One man meat is annada man poison
Yu can't tan pan cow back and cuss cow
Nuh use yu milk de cow and tun ova de bucket
Put yu brain inna gear
Before yu put yu mouth inna action
Bline can't lead bline
If yu cum fi drink milk nuh badda count cow
Wen yu deh a Rome yu do whey de Romans do
When trubble teck yu pickney shut fit yu
(Jack mandora mi nuh choose nun.)

NO MEDS

(Chorus)

Dem ah fia pure kappa, dem ah fia pure led
Dem ah shoot wan annada inna dem heads

De yutes now a day's nah whol nuh meds
Nah sey nuh praya before dem go ah dem beds
Den ah fia pure kappa, dem a fia pure led
Dem a shoot wan annada inna dem head
Dem a run de street, dem a run de street red
Can't buy nuh shuga, can't buy nuh bread
Dem ah truant fram school; nah obey de rule
Time to be wise, caan't behave like a fool
Pan de street karna dem smoking
Idling dem time just by skylarking
Dis type ah living lead to destruction
Dat nah help fi build de nation

(Chorus)

What is their goal and intention?
Betta get involved in some cultivation
Provide more food for de population
Help to uplift de negative condition
Alleviate de hardship and sufferation
De gross disrespect and violation
Caan't continue wid de speculation
Want improvement in de economic situation
Time fi get together an live as wan
Dat was how it were when dis earth began
Nuh badda wid nuh fus,
Nuh badda wid nuh fight
Let's get together and unite

(Chorus)

THE FUTURE

What does the future hold for us?
Are we prepared to face it without a fuss?
Every day we should acquire new skills
To learn to cope with difficulty and spills
In the normal course of our life
We have to face trials and strife

Reach out and grasp what you want
Don't just sit and wait
For someone else to do it for you
Take control of your own destiny
Make a move, get in the groove
Find ways to expand and improve.

Determination aids achievement,
No matter the situation
There's always a solution.
When everything seems to go wrong
Stand up; be strong so your days will be long
Concentrate, and put the pieces together

Make affirmations, be involved
Participate in activities, exude confidence
It all depends on you to take a stand
Your future is in your hand
Take it or leave it, it's all up to you
Whether you sink or float through

Every day we stand and stare
Living in a world without care
Are we blind? Can't we see?
What inactivity has done to us?
The vagrancies of life assail our minds
We seek yet we cannot find
The source of happiness and freedom
Life is just like sinking sand.

BACK A YARD

Ve va vup, ve va vup
Tea ta toe, tea ta toe
Which way to go?
I really don't know
Mi wuk so lang and hard
Time fi go back a mi yard.

I long for the exuberant sunshine
Wishing a life of bliss was mine
Prostrate in prayer on my knees
Picking a variety of fruits from the trees
The cool breeze blowing them to and fro
Long to eat some sweet mangoes

I long for the laughter of the village people
The music blaring in the vehicles
Farmers toiling in the hot sun
While children playing, having fun
Oh! How I miss my family and friends
Brethren and Sistren on the ends

TO MY ROOTS

I am going back to my Roots
My origin in the Gold Coast (West Africa)
From where my fore-parents
Were taken to the Caribbean and the Americas
To work on sugar and cotton plantations
Under the surveillance of Bactra Massa
With the crack of the whips across their backs
Working in the broiling sun from morn till dusk
Working every muscle and sinew
Goaded by the constant fear of physical abuse
Mothers and sisters deprived of their dignity

Oh! What a calamity on my ancestors
Instigated by the most ruthless oppressors
Deprived of their heritage, their roots, and language
Taken across the Atlantic on a triangular voyage
The most inhumane journey called the Middle Passage
Packed like commodity in the deep dungeons
For a life of misery, sufferation, and deprivation
But they couldn't kill the spirit of the African
Who stood resolute and strong to overcome
All indignation meted out to the one from creation.

QUESTIONS

Are you an able and enthusiastic member of the group?
Who takes keen interest and enjoys all aspects of the work?
Are you able to respond to a wide variety of stimulus material?
Including scripts of plays, pictures objects and images
Are you always willing and ready to plan and present ideas?
Through experimenting with others working cooperatively
Sensitively and flexibly working in a variety of groups
Showing commitment and initiative in achieving targets

Are you reliable, punctual, honest, and hardworking?
Striving to do your best at all times no matter the situation
We should seek to contribute to the development of the nation,
Working to create a successful career in life
Setting out your goals and aspirations
Charting your path to success as you advance
In the present, past, and the future
You are responsible for your success or failure

Attune your minds to the tasks at hand
Be prepared to work effectively to achieve your goals
Don't dither, never be a quitter
You can achieve whatever you want
Just make a start, play your part
Reach for the skies; you might just reach the clouds
When all around you is in turmoil
Be at peace with yourself
Rock the boat if you must but remain focused

BATTLE OF FALLUJAH

The battle of Fallujah
Let me hear you say Fallujah, Fallujah
What an atrocity pan the society

300,000 citizens told to evacuate or be shot
Systematic bombardment of their homes
By airplanes and helicopter gunships
Hospitals, religious, and educational institutions,
This is a wicked, dreadful situation
Patriots defending their country are called insurgents
Systematic murders of friends, neighbours, and relatives

The Battle of Fallujah
Let me hear you say Fallujah, Fallujah
What an atrocity pan de society

The mass media fabricates lies upon lies
To justify the wholesale slaughter of civilians
Women and children and old men
The agents of mass murder savage bombardment
Glorifying the heroism and success of their Elite Forces
Civilians are classified as terrorist sympathizers
Extermination of patriots defending their country
Fallujah is being raped and razed

Captured, wounded prisoners are shot in the Mosques
Food, water, and medicines are blocked from entering Fallujah
Wanton destruction of bridges and other infrastructure
Troops ordered to spray homes with machine guns
And tank fire before entering them
Acute malnutrition among young people
Has trebled since the US invasion
Open sewage water run on the streets
There is no electricity or cooking gas

The battle of Fallujah
Let me hear you say Fallujah, Fallujah
What an atrocity pan the society

LEARNING TO READ

Learning to read and express your ideas
Is vital for your literary and creative development
Make a concerted effort to learn
All the rudiments of reading
Spend time and expend maximum effort
To practice to read fluently and passionately
Read out aloud to friends,
Relatives and even strangers
Watch your features in a mirror,
Record your voice and listen to yourself
Your enunciation, pronunciation
And intonation is vital
In order to develop your confidence,
Boost your interest and widen your horizons
Grow your literary competences to the uttermost

Read from a wide variety of sources,
Expand your repertoire
Make it a natural habit so you will be comfortable
In expressing your ideas orally and in writing
Read for fun even when you are on the run
Read for pleasure and maximum enjoyment
It will ultimately lead to your advancement
Read for facts and information,
Gather evidence to substantiate
Make a valid conclusion
About people, places, and things
Make it a habit to travel
To near and distant places,
Get involved in mind-boggling
Experiences of writers, innovators
Photographers, thrill seekers like
Bungee jumping and mountain climbers

Expand your vocabulary;
Join a well-stocked library
Be an avid reader, a leader,
An innovator a creator of literary works
This can incite passion, take you on a mission
Take a trip to an unfamiliar destination
Discover the tantalizing, breathtaking experience
Delving in the mysteries of life
Through the pen of an amateur
Or professional enthusiast
Be grateful for your indulgence
As you expand your diligence
They say,
'Reading makes a full man or woman'
Fulfill the self-fulfilling prophecy
Embark on your rewarding discovery
Venture into the world of literary imagination.

EXOTIC JAHMECKYA

Jahmeckyah ah wan beautiful Island in de Caribbean
Look, listen learn an understand
Because ah Jahmeckyah mi cum fram
People cum fram whol heap ah countries
Fi experience de sights sea an sun
Soh cum along an hab some fun
Wi nuh hab pears and peaches
Wi hab de most exotic beaches

Wid 7 miles ah white sand beach inna Negril
Up de mountain, dung de valley den up the hill
Wi hab Dunns' River Falls, Reach an Whys' Falls
Go rafting pan de Rio Grande or Martha Braes Riva
Trodding de Mountains could mek yu shiver
Visit exotic places like Castleton Gardens
Wid ah variety of palm trees blowing in de breeze
Dere is Hope Gardens and Jahmeckyah House Gardens

Experience di picturesque Lovers Leap
Wid its breath taking enchanted peak
Cool off in de Guts Riva or de Alligator Pond Riva
Sip some refreshing, cool coconut jelly
Dem sey it good fi yu belly
If yu fancy a cool Red Stripe beer or wan Dragon Stout
Or betta still teck a taste of refreshing ginger beer
Fiery flavoured fi arouse yu taste buds

Savour some spicy Jerk Chicken
Dem deh food finger licking
Wid festival or roast yam ready fi n'aam
Or parched pounded corn called hassham
Don't feget de run-dung wid mackerel an banana
Or better still fi wi national dish, Ackee an Salt fish
Yu can get roast breadfruit or roast yam
Roast corn or fry dumpling fi n'aam
Wash dung wid manish wata

If yu preffa hot pepper shrimp from Lacovia
Or de savoury Boston Jerk pork fram Portland
Or a cool glass ah lemonade tingled wid
The flavour of Seville orenge
Hab some, pine apple, custard apple, or rose apple
Meck yu nuh try de tangy tamarind or jimbiling
Guava, June plums, sweet sop or sour sop
Nuh badda feget the wide variety of mangoes

Yu can savour de reggae music
Yu really can't refuse it
Wid 'Reggae Sum fest' inna Montego Bay
'Rebel Salute' near St Ann's Bay
'Saddle in de East' whey bearded man feast
Out in de west try 'Reggae Consciousness'
Decemba 26th; nuh fuss, nuh fight,
Peace and love wi bring
Just go ah Jam World fi 'Sting'

During de Independence Celebration
Visit Denbigh Show Grounds inna Clarendon
Wedda ah up town or dung town
Yu must visit Trench Town Culture Yard
Whey Bob Marley and the Wailers start
Fi record Reggae Music wid Joe Higgs
Tyrone Taylor watched de sunset
Fram a cottage in Negril

'Lambs bred' and 'Skunk' grow up ah 'Orenge Hill'
Tek ah leisurely ride through 'Holland Bamboo'
'Fern Gully' or even de 'Devils Race Course'
Den head fi de cool hills ah Portland
To Moore Town or Clarkes Town
Home of de legendary Nanny of the Maroons
Or Accompong Town inna northern St Elizabeth
Where Cudjoe signed de Peace Treaty
Wid Colonel Guthrie of de Red Coats

Trod outa Nine Miles to Bobbo Hill
Or betta still trod up to 'Pinnacle' inna Sligoville
De groundation fi Rastafarians
Visit 'Scots Pass Nyiah Binghi Center'
Pan de barder of Clarendon an Manchester
Whey nuh wicked can't enta
Tek a trod ova to 'Pit Four' inna Montego Bay

For your educational development visit
De University of de West Indies Mona Commons
Near August Town whey Bedward tried to fly
Dere is de Northern Caribbean University
Inna de cool hills ah Mandeville
Mico University College pan Marescaux Road
St Joseph Teachers College pan Old Hope Road
Short Wood Teachers College pan Short Wood Road

Moneague Teachers College inna Moneague
Bethlehem Teachers College inna Malvern St Elizabeth
Sam Sharpe Teachers College inna Montego Bay
College of Agriculture and Science Education
Inna Buff Bay Portland
Noh badda feget C.A.S.T.,
Now University of Technology
Pan Hope Road
De G C Foster Sports College
Inna Twickenham Park
Visit Edna Manley College of Performing Arts
For Art and Dancing pan Author Wint Drive
Whey singers and players of instruments come alive

De Institute of Jamaica pan East Street
Alongside Liberty Hall or Edelweiss Park,
Whey Marcus Garvey held Elocution contest
Don't forget the Vere Johns' 'Opportunity Hour'
At de Historic Ward Theatre inna Parade, Kingston
Fi wi Capital City whey things can be nitty an gritty
Suh much more fi sey but tune in annada day
Another time an place an
Jahmeckya no Problem, Ebbery ting Irie,
One Love Jam Dung.

Jamaica   No problem

COURAGE

C is for Confidence, an enduring quality we must emulate
O is for Outstanding, something to strive for
U is for Understanding your purpose in life
R is for Responsibility, responding positively in all situations
A is for Advancement, boldly advancing towards our goal
G is for Gratitude, being thankful for the things in life
E is for Excellence, excelling to the highest level

RESPONSIBILITY

R is for Respecting each other
E is for Excellence, that which we must strive for
S is for Special, unique, one of a kind
P is for Purpose our role in life
O is for Oneness working together as one
N is for Novelty bringing something different
S is for Support to each and everyone
I is for Intelligence utilizing your talents
B is for Bravery advancing to your goal
I is for Interest paying maximum attention
L is for Love the most precious commodity
I is for Internal getting to know yourself
T is for Tangible, real and authentic
Y is for Youth, forever staying fresh and vibrant.

TAKING A STAND

We cannot continue like this,
It seems like something has gone amiss
Why should we just exist, when there
Is more than enough for all of us?
To live to the full extent of our potential
And realize our dreams
This situation cannot be perpetuated
We must refuse to be contained,
Restrained or manipulated
Let us rearrange our activities
And sort out the priorities
Forge ahead with grit and determination
In order to bolster ourselves
From this dreadful situation

Make a difference in the scheme of things
Take a pro-active approach to direct events
Accelerate the pace of life to achieve desired results
Organize and centralize to realize the stated objectives
Accomplish the mission statement and raise the stakes
Accelerate the impetuous to produce the resources
To move forward in earnest to establish the product
To build the solid foundation
For our economic livelihood

For too long we have been left behind to do menial tasks
Never in charge of the production methods used to advance
The economic ventures that have positioned nations
To be technologically advanced and control the reins
Of power; militarily, politically economically, and socially
The time has come when we must rise up in one accord
With a burning desire to make a difference in the society
Taking control, leading the charge of our own destiny.

FROM THE INVESTIGATOR

The same fire that melts the butter hardens the egg
Habit is like a cable, we weave a thread of it every day
Until it becomes so strong that we cannot break it
Attitude is the aroma of your heart.
If your attitude stinks it means your heart is not right.
Don't quit; keep going on and on,
Winners never quit, quitters never win
If you want something go for it;
Be smart and go for it.
If you are short—stand on the shoulders
Of giants to gain your advantage

Focus is the key ingredient to your success;
Settle for more not less
Concentrate on the window of success;
Take time to reflect
It's all in your state of mind,
Seek and you will find the elixir of life
Activate your sensory receptors,
Be enthusiastic, punctual, and dependable
Have faith in self, have faith in others,
Get up and face it and not be distracted.

DETERMINATION

When all odds are stacked against you
Don't give up, move on, and be strong
For yourself; your family and friends
Even with the last ounce of energy
Will yourself forward to your goal
Never surrender, never retreat
Move your hands and feet
Urge yourself to achieve
To realise your desire

Don't sit and wait for events to unfold
Be warm and caring not cold
Life is not always a bed of roses
It's full of thistles and thorns
Realise your full potential
Get up, stand up, and be strong
When you reach your last tether
When the going gets tough
Let the toughness gets going
Be resilient and strong.

MY STORIES—READ AND REMINISCE

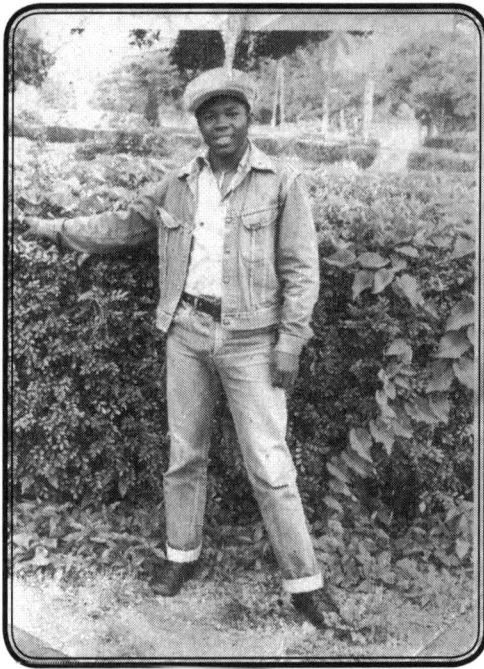

To all my classmates and friends from the village of Rock River and surrounding areas like Diamond, Simon, Suttons, Coxswain, Lime Hall, Mitchells Hill, Low Ground, and Morris Hall.

REMINISCENT OF MY SCHOOL DAYS

Exciting though they were, I have forgotten much of my school days. The experiences that I can easily recall are those that have made an indelible impression on my mental faculty. Rock River All Age School has played a very important part in my early upbringing. It was there that my formal education began under the illustrious and distinguished Head Teacher Mr. C.N. Greenwood. I can vividly recall as if it was yesterday how Teacher Greenwood used to stand at the school gate to spot latecomers. It was a rouse of ours to quicken our steps whenever we were in the precincts of the school gate to impress our Headmaster (affectionately called 'Chickum' by us on account of his regular coughing) that we were conscious of our lateness. He was a very strict disciplinarian who would never overlook a mistake. We had to dot all the i's and crossed all the ts.

At 'Break Time', we would rush to the various vendors at the school gate to purchase a variety of delicacies like coconut drops, gizaada, fried dumpling, fritters, bulla cake, red herring, crackers, and a wide variety of fruits in the season. There would be a constant shout as everyone would be ordering at the same time. We would then play cricket with 'bunker bat' (a kind of bat made from the coconut bough)—usually (ketchy shovie) whoever gets the ball would bowl or throw it depending on the type of ball we were using. It was quite exciting and we had fun playing to our hearts content in those days in the hills of Rock River.

There were the days when we get a chance of playing real cricket with proper gears compliments of the Community Sports Club led by M. Louden. C.N Greenwood would be the umpire and we had to impress him with our batting, bowling, and fielding. The other students would come out to watch along with the teachers and sometimes other members of the community.

Prominent among them was S. Campbell whom we affectionately call 'Sam Cutter' on account of his running commentaries. He would be present on the truck that took the Rock River Cricket team to various locations from near or far; places like Moores, Wood Hall, Chapelton, and Morgan's Pass. Those days were wonderful as we had a real sense of community spirit. I have embalmed those days and will tell my children, my grand—and great-grandchildren these old-time stories.

SPITFIRE INCORPORATION

Ladies and gentlemen, you are cordially welcome to Spitfire Incorporation.

Your wish is our command; whatever you say that we will obey. We are here to supply your every need. Just think of it and it will be yours. No obligations; I declare to you, nothing to pay today, tomorrow, next month, next year, or in the near future. The sky is the limit, just name it, we will supply your request. A luxurious life with an attractive wife by your side, girls at your behest twenty-four seven like you are in heaven. You have come to the right place at the right time. In the next thirty minutes, your every wish is my command. Whatever you want from a pin to an anchor, don't be shy. Your express wish will be granted with the utmost speed and precision. In a split second, immediately if not before, we can make your decision, gold, silver, diamond, or platinum; just state your desire and it will be granted by Spitfire Incorporation, nothing to pay, today, tomorrow, next month, next year, or in the near future.

I am Mr Spitfire, Managing Director and Central Executive Officer of the worlds' number one franchise of luxury and wealth, including fast cars, beautiful girls, race horses, casinos, hotels, diplomas and bachelors in education degrees, doctorate, fame, and fortune. Just sign on the dotted line, no obligations, nothing to pay, today, tomorrow, next month, next year, or for a long time. So come, don't be shy; just sign on the dotted line and you will be fine. Have you ever thought of fame and fortune, the Midas's touch? Good luck is my name. Your wish is my command.

Whatever you say, I'll obey; nothing to pay, today, tomorrow, next month, next year, or for a long time to come.

IT'S BETTER TO LIVE IN THE COUNTRY

'I will lift up my eyes to the hills from whence cometh my help'

Country life can be great fun, meaningful, and rewarding. Waking up in the misty morning, walking in the dew, inhaling the fresh air, hearing the chirping of the birds and insects, diving in the cool pool, picking fruits, gathering firewood, or raking the brown leaves also listening to the pitter-patter of the rain beating on the galvanized roof accentuate the wonders of country life.

More and more, people are now gravitating to the rural areas to establish residencies after a hectic life in the city. They want to take it easy and relax in the cool countryside closer to nature where most of our fruits and vegetables are produced. St Elizabeth on the South Coast is regarded as the bread-basket of our blessed island Jamaica, the land of wood and water.

Country folks are very affable, productive, and hospitable. Most of our export crops are from the country areas. Our rivers have their origins in the hills and percolates to the seas. Our quiet country folks are really the backbone of our country. Several of our most outstanding personalities in the field of politics, sports, education, and culture have their origin in the country area. Many of our heroes, including Marcus Garvey from St Ann's Bay, Alexander Bustamante from Hanover, Norman Manley from Manchester, and Paul Bogle from St Thomas.

Our athletes, Merlene Ottey from Hanover, Usain Bolt from Trelawney, Sandy Richards from Clarendon, just to name a few. Our musicians, Bob Marley from Nine Miles St Anne, also Burning Spear also from St Anne, Beres Hammond from St Mary, Jimmy Cliff from St James, Cocoa Tea, Everton Blender, and Freddy McGregor from Clarendon. Jamaica's first female Prime

Minister Portia Simpson Miller from St Catherine, Minister of Foreign Affairs A. J. Nicholson from Clarendon, Minister of Agriculture and Fisheries Roger Clarke, and former Prime Minister P. J. Patterson from Westmoreland.

With the proliferation of motor vehicles, telephone services, Rural Electrification Programme, the rapid expansion of the water services by the National Water Commission, the record-breaking pace of construction of houses by the National Housing Trust, the upgrading, construction, and expansion of schools. The University of the West Indies, 'Distance Teaching Programme', along with Community Colleges, construction of highways, rationalization of the health sector has surely helped to regenerate the country areas to be more desirable and competitive. Hundreds of thousands of our nationals who send remittances from abroad are from the country areas like Farm Workers, Immigrants from England, North, South and Central America and many islands in the Caribbean are mostly country folks.

With all of the above said, it is clear that it is better to live in the country than in the town.

A DAY OF FISHING

Fishing was one of my favourite past times. Whenever I went fishing, my first catch usually occurred quickly. On this occasion, I fished a long time before I had any success. It was a sunny Sunday morning when the grass was saturated with the night dew that I decided to go fishing. My knapsack was carefully packed, and I set off with my rod and line to the Rio Minho River. The journey was uneventful; the chirping of birds and the silent crush of the bamboo leaves as I trod through the bamboo grove were the only signs of life.

On reaching the river, I took up my position on a large rock under a massive gwango tree near a deep pool of water as blue as the sky over which hung several bamboo trees bowing as if in prayer. I let out my line, baited it, threw it into the cool water, and sat contentedly waiting for some sign of a bite. The whole place was very quiet. It seemed as if I was alone in the world. The water was static; the air was still with an eerie calmness yet gave a feeling of peace and tranquillity.

Suddenly, the breeze began to blow as the bamboo trees swayed to and fro. I watched my line for some sign of movement but noticed that it remained still. After a while I drew it and noticed that the bait was still intact. I looked at it with an expert's eye and realised that it was not touched. I decided to move to another spot. This time I sat on a piece of log which hung over the water and sheltered by a huge rose apple tree. I sat patiently and silently for a very, very long time, but still there was no sign of a bite. This forced me to move to another spot, this time under a slender trumpet tree, but still I did not get a bite. It seemed that the fishes were on a holiday.

I came to the conclusion that I was wasting my time and decided to pack up and head for home. Just then, I saw a ripple on the water's surface. This renewed my interest. I moved in that direction and threw my line. Finally, I saw some sign of a bite. My heart was now beating faster. I placed my hand on the rod and waited anxiously. Suddenly, there was a big jerk and I felt the line getting taut. I began to wind in the spindle and felt something struggling to get off. My whole system was now on full alert as I exerted some more pressure and began to wind in the line. The rod, being a flexible one, began to bend as if it would break. I took hold of the line itself and after a gruelling struggle managed to put my catch ashore. It was a real beauty, a big glistening mullet with its gill dripping blood and moving in a menacing way. It weighed about five pounds. I deposited it in my knapsack and commenced my journey home. I will never forget that memorable Sunday.

DESTRUCTION OF BOBBY'S HOUSE

It was a custom of ours to occupy Bobby's half-finished house under the embankment around Broken Bank below Mrs Penny's 'Haunted House', used as a recluse by us. Bobby's real name was L. James, affectionately called Little John or just simply Bobby.

On this luckless day, I happened to just jaunt on the precincts of Mrs Binta or Operator as she was fondly called because of her habit of charging us five cents to watch her television, which was the only one in our area. I behold Percy, Winky, and Cooter in a contest of stoning Bobby's house. I asked them if they were mad, and told them to desist from damaging the house. They paid no heed and continued more relentlessly to damage the galvanised roof.

At this opportune time, who should chance to pass by but Allan Brown called by us as A.B. 42 D6 because of his industrious habit of forking a huge amount of land in a very short time. He started to curse indecent language and utter other profanities. As by design, who should come bopping along but D.C. Donald, kack ye'ye Donald from Mullet Hall? He said, 'Mr Brown, I'm going to arrest you for using indecent language.' Mr Brown stuttered, 'I ma-eh eh ah—ah dem rause bway yaw a lick dung Bobby's house.' Donald interrupted him, 'Mi noh care what yu sey but mi ah go prosecute you.'

All this time, we just watched and cheered. Without any further ado, Allan Brown jumped off the bank and positioned himself on top of Little John's stone heap, took up two big stones, and stuttered, 'Co—co come down yaw so meck a bruck yu up.' Donald started to walk towards him and he dropped the stones and ambled through the orange orchard and went over his yard. Donald said, 'all right, Missa Brown, I'm going for the baton and badge' (In those days when a D.C.—District Constable—wears his badge and has a baton, he was a VIP.).

Within a short time, Donald returned swinging the baton in his right hand and exhibiting the D.C. badge on his right shirt sleeve shoulder. He passed us briskly and went to AB 42 D6 gate and started to call loudly, 'Missa Brown, a come to arrest you in the name of the law for using indecent language and resisting arrest.' AB 42 D6 did not answer. He crept quietly under the bed and kept silent. Mrs Brown became agitated and started to implore her husband to go out to the D.C. She said, 'Mr Brown come out from under the bed for me nuh want nuh trouble, see the D.C. with the baton and the badge,' but Mr Brown kept still.

After a while, Donald left and the place was very quiet. Mr Brown inquired from under the bed, 'Him gawn?' Misses Brown replied in a hushed voice, 'Yes him gawn long time.' He then scrambled from under the bed shrouded with cobweb and dirt. Mrs Brown interspersed, 'Mr Brown you were fretting?' Mr Brown replied, 'A—ah—ah miss's.'

The next day, Donald served him a summon, for which he went to court and paid twenty dollars—'serves him right'. When I saw Little John the next day, he said, 'Tro-poh fauth man; mi think me an onno was friends, me just a come from up a Mrs Elanor mi tell her piece a mi mind, mi ah go dung a Almighty Bones go tell him the other piece now.'

The next time I saw Little John he said, 'Fi mi man oh onno nuh go dung a yard go play nuh more cashew yah sah, far police ah go sweep oono up.'

'Ah Yah Yah, Jack mandora mi nuh choose nun.'

FIRST CLASS TEST

In a remote district called Suttons in North Central Clarendon on the Island of Jamaica, there lived a family of three: Mass Ashley the father, Miss Bettie the mother, and Sunny the son. Sunny used to dress up every evening and dutifully go up to Four Paths to count cars or just feast his eyes on passing girls. He didn't really have a girlfriend, although from time to time he would make presents of oranges, mangoes, pears, star apples, or custard apples from his father's vineyard to many girls in the district who would just make fun of him.

Whenever the Annual Clarendon College Fair was held in Chapelton, Sunny would be there dressed in his 'Sunday best' but never went inside. He was always outside looking in and dancing to the beat of the music.

He was an eccentric one, with bulging eyes, large hands, and a silly grin on his face. It happened that Sunny got a 'Farm Work Card' and went for the Fitness Test at the Denbigh Show Grounds, and guess what? Sunny passed the test. When Sunny reached home, the news of his exploits reached the district before him. When his father saw him, he ran and embraced him and kissed him on his cheek and said, 'Sunny, you passed the test?' Sunny replied, 'Yes pappa, ah pass the test.' Mass Ashley said, 'My son, Sunny passed the test, it is a first class test, this calls for a celebration. Sunny come with me, we are going down to Miss Tiny Shop to buy a few items for the celebration.' On their way to the shop, they were greeted by many people who had heard the news. They congratulated Sunny for his success, shaking his hands and wishing him all the best.

On reaching the shop, Mass Ashley strutted boldly up to the counter and said in a loud and commanding voice with a broad smile on his face, 'Good evening, Miss Cissy, sell me one pound of mixed flour, pound and a half of sugar, half pound of salt, big gill coconut oil, see the bottle here, and two Red Stripe beer. I am having a celebration tonight and you are all invited. My son Sunny passed a test. It is a first class test.' People hear about it from north, south, east, and west

Miss Tiny interjected, 'What kind of test did Sunny pass, after Sunny not going to any school?'

Mass Ashley responded, 'Now, now, Miss Cissy, imagine that you are an outstanding person in the community, running this grocery shop and you don't hear the news? It is the commonest talk around here, people over in Rock River, which is three and a half miles from here, people in Chapelton, May Pen, Tommy King, Pennants, Cupits, and Summerfield. In fact, people from all over talking about it. Get up to date Miss Cissy, get up-to-date. Get information about what is happening in the nation. You should be ashamed of yourself. Get up to date.'

When the white man tested him hand, him say, 'Young man, you are fit as a fiddle. Will you work seven days per week and eat pork for breakfast, lunch, and dinner?' Sunny said, 'Yes sir, I will even work eight days per week and eat pork seven days per week if you say so, sir. Mi wi even eat the grunt and the rope if you gimmie dem, sir.'

'My son Sunny doesn't eat meat, him don't drink milk, him don't smoke, and he has never been with a woman, so him must be strong. When my son goes on the Farm Work, all I want him to bring for me is a transistor radio, so I can listen di news. Ah gwine baps it ah mi ears and listen di RJR News.'

Sunny went on the Farm Work and only spend one week; a bawl sey him want go home for America too cold. The supervisors sent Sunny back to Jamaica quickly on account of his constant complaint. When Mass Ashley reaches the airport, he said, 'Sunny how you come back so quickly? Some young men stay for weeks, even months, or for a whole year, how you come back so quickly.' Sunny replied softly, 'Pappa, mi did cold and want come home, mi miss you and mamma and everybody.' Mass Ashley said, 'Come meck wi go home, you will have to plant cassava yam and banana, and all kinds of ground provision, you lazy brute.'

(Jack mandora mi nuh choose none.)

VISIONS OF THE PAST

I woke up with a start, having a vision of the past, visualising my mother washing clothes, laughing, scrubbing, and spreading them to dry on the sandstones on the banks of the Rio Minho River. I can vividly recall being placed in a tub sheltered from the rays of the burning sun by wild cane leaves or bamboo trees swaying in the breeze. We were not alone as there were Aunty Dora, Aunty Seta, Aunty Luna, and Aunty Roslyn—all chatting and laughing as they scrub the clothes on the flat rock sodden by 'cake soap' (a type of soap made from crude bits of coconuts, acids, and other stuff from Seprod Manufacturing Company in Kingston off Spanish Town Road).

Picking coffee beans, planting corns, peanuts, or reaping tobacco leaves were some of the tasks my mother and the other ladies were engaged in for 'Tanimo. He was a whale of a man who had a huge tobacco house at North Hall. This was made from bamboo and coconut boughs perched on a massive swathe of flat alluvial soil rich in the silt washed down when the river overflows its banks on a seasonal pattern. Tanimo didn't have a wife, sweetheart, or any children to cook food for him. He would usually drink a whole tin of Betty or Nestles' sweetened condensed milk from the tin or pour it out on stale bread that he usually get from Mr Chin, who was his banker. He used this stale bread to feed his massive hogs that he kept in a sturdy bamboo sty. I am able to recall this clearly as I used to collect the tin wrappers that had pictures and information about the wide variety of birds in Jamaica like the John—to wit, Robin Red Breast, Doctor Bird, Goose Finch, Banana-Katie, Chick Man Chick, Wood Pecker, Parakeet, Grass Quit, Beanie Bud, Bald Plate, Barbell Dove, Ground Dove, Partridge, White Belly, White wing, and Pitcheary.

As a boy growing up in the rural district of Suttons and then Rock River, going to the rivers and woodlands around were very exciting. We used to catch fish with our bare hands or use fishing lines with hook line and sinker attached to a slim line bamboo pole or a wild cane rod. We would also use mesh wire to make stream pots which we worked as a team to entrap the fishes, mostly African perch, crayfish, or shrimps. We would sometimes set fish pots overnight which we would visit in the fresh morning air, walking in the grass wet with dew and our toes filled with the moist soil on the river bank.

In those days, the Rio Minho was a vibrant river flowing swiftly and teemed with a wide variety of fishes. In the rainy season, it was a massive force to be reckoned with overflowing its banks and carrying away livestock and vast acreages of land under cultivation. It was fun for us as we did not realise the dangerous nature of this natural force. We would ride the torrents on logs and bamboo pole, laughing and frolicking in the ebb and flow of the treacherous river, salvaging a variety of farm products like bunches of plantains or bananas, dry coconuts, livestock, and fruits on trees or other goodies. Looking back now, it was so much fun and excitement as we braved the waves and flexed our muscles against the forces of nature and living off the fruits of our labour in the hills of North Central Clarendon on the wonderful Island of Jahmeckyah.

TRO-TRO POW-POW

Long ago when mi y'eye deh ah mi knee, mi used to wear short trousers and mi foot sole grounded, mi used to visit mi granny an mi grand pa. When evening come granny put on the big Yabba pot and fills it with earth food. Mi notice the absence of salting so mi sey, Granny yu nah cook nuh salting? Mi granny scratch her head and sey, 'Son, ah only we two lib, mi and you grand pa. When mi cook the likkle bickle wi just ny'aam it so, so, so. Yu grand pa preffa fi save up the money in ah the big calabash.'

Last week, mi really want fi test him so when Sunday m'awning come mi get up bright and early and look after him favourite breakfast, bammy and chocolate tea broiling hot with de oil pan de top, but mi nuh put one drop a sugar in deh. Mi set it pan the table and call him. Him bless it and start savour the taste. When him reach halfway through it mi hear him sey, 'Rachel di tea could teck likkle bit more sugar.' Mi sey, 'Den granny him really drink it without sugar.' She sey, 'A soh him used to it so—soh soh.'

Granny sey, 'Anyway mi noh know if like how you deh yah him wi do any betta. Go dung a gully and tell him fi give yu tro-pance meck yu buy tro-pance shad.' So mi hop skip and jump till mi reach de guinep tree trunk whey him a sharpen him belly woman cutlass and sey. 'Gr-aan pa, gra—granny s-ey fi gi mi tro-pance—m-ek mi buy t-rop-ance shad.' Him look up wid a frown an wipe him forehead wid him big finga. Mi utterance seem fi startle him, for him raise himself up and look mi straight in a mi 'yeye and sey, 'Tropance shad! Wholla tro-pance shad? Yu a go uppen shap? Bwaay you mad? Look how tro-pance shad nuff?' Grand pa sey, 'Anyway tell her fi look ova de creng-creng him see de dutchy wid some oil kibba up wid coco leaf whey mi use last week, him fi go dung a di tro-tro patta and pick two big tro-tro, she fi cook dem till dem soft and meck tro—tro pow—pow. An mi grand pa nebba tap 'naam tro—tro pow—pow till him deaf.'

Ah yah yah!

THE DAY MY CAP WAS TAKEN

Growing up with my mother in the deep rural hills of Suttons Clarendon was very exciting and memorable. I remember it as if it was yesterday. Wearing a cap was one of my favourite attire, and I cherished the caps that Aunty Beryl made for me or the ones I got from my father, who would send a parcel or barrel occasionally especially on Christmas holidays.

Mr Herman Walters had a small shop at the bottom of Ennis Hill (our skating rink, the hill we rode our skating contraption on). He had several mongrel dogs that would yap continuously at us when we were passing on the North Hall Road. There was a fortified bamboo fence through which we would poke the dogs with pointed sticks mischievously. We would then run away as soon as they started to yelp and howl from the piercing point of our sticks. This continued for several weeks until Miss Cissy, Mr Walters's partner, caught us in the act and reported the matter to Mr Wallace who was a tall dark and lanky man with piercing eyes like the chicken hawks that he usually shoots down at North Hall near 'Bud Cave', mostly during the bird shooting season. He had a long double-barrelled Remington with an ivory butt which he hung over his long shoulder with the barrel broken back.

Mr Walters was a specimen of a man you don't joke with. He would watch out for you whenever you go to buy groceries and intimidate you with his glaring hawk-like eyes and long hands as he stood seven feet tall. There was a sweet, sweet guinep tree next to the front of the shop that we used to raid. We would mostly use a crutch stick to pick the juicy bunches of guinep of fling stones at them then pick up the pods which we would suck off the seed as they were sweet like wet sugar. Sometimes we would even chew up the seeds and swallow the sweet bits.

On this particular sunny Sunday morning, Mass Enos and I were going to Martha Hole to do some fishing. Martha Hole was one of the deepest, bluest holes in the river. We had our bamboo fishing rods slung over our shoulders with our lines carefully entwined. We stopped at Mass Wallace's shop to buy 'tro pance' worth of Chins' bulla cake to eat with some succulent avocado pear that we had saved for the occasion. We also bought 'quatty' worth of brown sugar and a plastic bag of ice to mix with Seville orange.

While Miss Cissy was wrapping the sugar I went over the guinep tree to pick some to eat. I used my bamboo rod which had a small crutch at the top to pick a big bunch of guinep. The stem snapped and I tried to catch it but it fell to the ground and scattered all over the place. Unawares that I was been watched by the mongrel dogs I started to pick up the guinep and heard the dogs growling menacingly. Suddenly a big brown bull dog silently pounced on me and held me down with his front paws and snatched my cap and retreated under the fence with my cap in his barring teeth. I was taken by surprise and felt a shiver of fear crept up my spine causing me to tremble like a leaf. When I regained my composure I took up a big stone and hurled it with all my might in the direction where the dog went. The other dogs came to the fence to fend off my advance. There was a great commotion as the dogs barked and yelped at me for intruding on their territory. I retreated hastily from the treat of the advancing beasts.

Mr Walters emerged from the front room and stood imposingly on the veranda. He looked at me with anger on his face and his eyes were red with rage. I stuttered almost inaudibly, 'The big brown bull dog took my cap under the fence.' 'Serves you right,' he said in a firm tone of voice. 'Every day you tease those dogs, you throw stones at them, and you even poke them with pointed sticks. When they howl and squeal in pain you run and laugh and think it is fun.' It was the first time that I had seen Mass Walters with a smirk of smile on his coarse, taut lanky face. I felt humiliated and dejected. I didn't bother to retrieve my cap and beat a hurried retreat from the vicinity as the altercation had attracted several onlookers. Mass Enos said, 'Come bredda Jim, mek we go a river.' I didn't need any prompting as I was leading the way slinking like a beaten tramp out of sight. I shall never forget to remember that hapless Sunday morning when the big, brown bull dog took my cap.

MYSELF AS A WAITER

The North Hall Hotel started off as a simple and exotic hotel catering to the culinary needs of the local villagers, who were looking for a place to meet and greet each other in a secure and quiet environment. Eight years had passed very quickly since I have been employed at the hotel. I have given tremendous service which has helped its growth and development for it to become a beacon of prosperity. Those who came to dine were treated with the best hospitality possible and these customers returned on a regular basis. In view of my position, I met many distinguished personalities. The regular customers knew me as a competent, considerate, and reliable waiter who adhered to rules and regulations.

One day, an old woman came into the hotel. She was poorly dressed. Her shoes were only a fragment of what they were. Her dress—if you could call it dress—was tattered and badly needed sewing. Her hair was grey and her cheeks were lean and taut, and it seemed as if she was suffering from malnutrition. Her appearance had an effect on me and this forced me to be compassionate to her. I gave her the best there was although she could not pay for it. She ordered the cheapest and least nutritious meals. My heart was full of so much compassion—oblivious to the fact that I was doing the wrong thing. This happened on several occasions.

A few months later, a young man of about thirty-years-old acquired the hotel. He called me to his office and told me what he had learnt from the old woman, and how I was giving away the food. He even told me that the old woman was his mother, and since she had the most shares in the business, he would have to do what she said. He went on to say that she had firmly stated that I should be replaced by a more reliable and astute person.

For a moment, I was rooted to the spot. It was as if I was bewitched. I could hardly believe what I had just heard. I thought I had imagined it, but seeing the proprietor standing before me, I knew it was real. I had allowed my compassion to overcome me, and now I was going to lose my job. I did not try to explain in any way to the proprietor. I had learnt my lesson but in future, I feel if the same situation should arise, I would not hesitate to do it all over again.

AN UNFORTUNATE SITUATION

The black Mercedes Benz was stalking him like a panther. Suddenly the cold hackneyed morning was shattered by the ra-ta-ta-ta—of a machine gun. Bob was hit at point-blank range and was dead instantly like a doornail. The ambulance came and took his emaciated body to Homerton Hospital, where a ferocious mob converged to exact revenge. They were out to create mayhem, as Bob was a fond member of the community.

Luckily, the police came and managed to diffuse the situation. They re-assured the seething mob that CCCTV had caught the license plate of the getaway car and the gunman was apprehended in Clapton Pond, after a furious chase by a zealous pair of young police officers who were alerted. The crowd dispersed reluctantly and some were agitated and spoke of exacting their own form of justice.

As if by design, a horde of reporters from several media houses were quick on the scene to cover the unfortunate incident. Cameras were flashing rapidly and several microphones were thrust at the most vocal set of people. Prominent among them was a tall burly built Rasta man with chunky flowing locks flashing in the wind. He spoke in rapid tones in the Jamaican lingua with his facial muscles knitted and eyes bulging as if he was about to explode. He drawled these words in a deliberate way, 'Dem yah bway don't care a backside, dem a behave like sey dem can mek life. Dem should lack dem up fi life. Imagine if it was my son dem shat. Police would haffe lack mi up. Yu tink sey it wudda go so—so so. No sah, nat at all.'

MY RECOLLECTIONS

Our father had migrated to England and my mother was under pressure to take care of my sister Junita, affectionately called Putus, my brother Ralph, and myself. Putus was named by my mother's father James Carridice (Daddy) from whom I got my name. It was decided that I would go to live with one of my father's sister in Rock River. My brother Ralph was sent to live with his grandmother (Granny) up Ennis Hill and my sister Putus would join our father in England.

I recall vividly the day I packed my scant belongings in a small carton box and set off on my journey through the lush vegetation on the North Hall road across the Rio Minho, accompanied by my sister Putus. It was a very hazardous journey through rough footpaths hewn through rocks and forest by the hoofs of sturdy donkeys. On reaching 'Ten Mile' or Tanarchy where the footpath joined the main road from May Pen, we stopped at Aunty Gladys's shop to get some refreshment of 'bulla cake and avocado pear' which was washed down with ice cold lemonade. We then proceeded on our journey to Rock River to my aunt's residence. It was a warm reception. When my sister was ready to leave, tears flooded my eyes. She comforted me and assured me that I would soon settle down. I was surrounded by several cousins who made me feel at home. I soon resigned myself to the reality that this was to be my home, the place I would have to stay from now until I was able to fend for myself. From that day, I made a resolution that I must survive no matter the trials and tribulations. There was an Anglican Church right opposite our home by the name of St James Mission. It was from this caption that I soon learn to write my name. Church going was a compulsory affair for us as we were the ones who had to sweep the church, arrange the seats, spread up the tables, ring the bell, and undertake every activity that was relevant to its smooth running.

I remember accompanying my sister to the Palisades Airport now Norman Manley International Airport. It was my first visit to an airport and I was very excited. I gazed and gazed at the tall buildings and looked with awe at the sights that were unfolding before my eyes. My mother took my sister to the check-in counter where her luggage was checked and weighed in. We heard an announcement over the loudspeaker. I looked in amazement, my sister kissed us, and said goodbye and walked along a long passage with other passengers. My mother ushered me to the waving gallery. I saw several people on the flight of steps going up the airplane, soon I saw my sister. She waved to us, and I felt the tears running down my cheeks like water gushing from a tap. I became hysterical and began to climb the metal fence that separates us. I could faintly hear my mother telling me to stop crying. She wiped my eyes, and as I looked the door of the airplane was closed and the steps were taken away. The engine of the airplane began to be revved up and after a while the airplane started to move slowly, gathered speed, taxied down the runway rapidly, and soared in the air with a roar as loud as thunder. I watched it until it went over the horizon and out of sight. There was a hollow feeling in my belly; a part of me was gone, gone in the wind. My mother took my hand and said, 'Come, Brother Jim, "Put" gawn, come mek wi go home.' I will always remember that day when my sister left for England.

PUTUS IN ENGLAND

I missed my family whom I was leaving behind, but I was determined to give it a try. I had several sleepless nights pondering and wondering what it would be like in England. My mother was very busy looking about my passport, making several trips to May Pen and Kingston. It was very exciting for me as my friends at school knew that I would be going to England and really treated me with respect. I basked in it while it lasted, for very soon this turned into jealousy as I was leaving them behind and going to a faraway land where the snow fell in winter and leaves faded off the trees as the place was cold as ice.

As I ascended the plane steps and waved to my mother and brother, my mind was in a swirl. I was leaving my home and family to go to a faraway place where I knew no one. The journey was uneventful. I soon fell asleep as I did not sleep for two nights before. I awoke several hours later and was given some food and drink, which I only ate a little of as it tasted different from the type of food I was used to. After what seemed like eternity, we finally reached Heathrow Airport. I was one of the first one to be escorted off the BOAC plane and taken to the arrival desk wearing my blue anorak coat which my father had sent for me a few weeks before.

I didn't really know my father so well and he didn't know me so well either as we didn't grow up with him. He would travel to England and then return to Jamaica and had a room in Rock River.

I was met at the airport by my dad and his friend who accompanied him. He had sent the blue anorak coat for me to wear so that he could identify me easily. He recognised me and proceeded to question me about my mother and grandparents' name. I was able to give prompt responses which brought laughter to his cheeks and with a warm embrace he welcomed me to England. We left the airport and made our first stop in Finsbury Park where my brother and sister lived. Their mother was not at home and we were not allowed to go inside. My dad and I spoke to them for a while then we left for Wolverhampton. It was an uneventful journey and I slept most of the way as I was jetlagged.

On reaching Wolverhampton, I was awakened by my father who said, 'Putus, we reach.' My scant belongings were taken from the trunk of the car and brought into the house. There was a fire burning in the fireplace and the house felt warm and cozy. My mother-in-law greeted me with a bright smile and a warm hug and showed me a room which I had to share with my sisters. After eating my dinner of gungo peas soup with salt beef, yellow yam, and corn meal dumplings, and drinking a cup of water, I went upstairs and fell in a deep sleep. I will always remember that day.

My sister Junita affectionately called (Putus)

AN ENCOUNTER WITH ROLAND PILE

One Friday morning, I was going to school in Rock River; on reaching the square I stopped with some friends to wait for classmates who were coming on the 'Doreen Bus' which plied the route from Reckford to May Pen every day, except Sundays. While I was there, I saw Brother Robinson the street sweeper doing his usual rounds. Part of my hobby was calling people nicknames and Brother R was not too fond of me for I really irritate him on many occasions by calling him a string of names, e.g., Fisherman trunk and A Soono. He got the name fisherman trunk on account of his big belly and the name A Soono on account of his accent of talking up in his nose. Brother R was a whale of a man and walked with a limp. He usually rides a bicycle and was always accompanied by several underfed dogs. You didn't have to say the words 'Fisherman trunk' to get him upset; you merely had to purse you lips and whistle them.

This particular Friday morning, I felt bold and confronted Brother R and said,

'Hey, Brother R, me a big man now and mi stop run from you. Mi a go stop call you nickname and me nuh fraid a yu again.' I could feel my adrenalin rushing through my body making me feel flushed and hot. I was dressed in my khaki suit and had my bag over my shoulder. There was a hush and several children began to gather around. Brother R said, 'All right, you a big man now, tan up deh meck a ketch yu.' He ambled towards me and I walked slowly towards Hepburn McLeod's shop and stood up to face him. When he realized that I was serious, he slowly retreated and continued with his sweeping and mumbled under his breath. 'Wait till a ketch yu man, yu just wait till a ketch yu man, ah gwine mek yu know whey wata walk go a pumpkin belly.'

A crowd of children looked on excitedly anticipating some more fun-filled excitement.

Who should come along to confront me but 'Roland Pile', one of my regular nicknamee. Roland Pile got his name from a pile he had, a boson or swelling of his testicles. He was a specter of a person—short in stature, with a white ram goat beard, long and taut jaw bone, teeth like Kong dog, long and crumpled trousers which he had to roll up on his ankles. His shirt tail was long and reached down to his knocked knees; his foot soles were grounded and were cracked so wide you could plant corn grain in them. His toes were long and crusty, and the nails were long and looked tough like fi chicken hawk. He had a dirty string bag over his greasy shirt and a little dull curvy, dirty-looking knife attached to a soiled piece of string about one foot long. Some of his nicknames were ma-bell sow, cane piece rat, and ram goat beard. Out of nowhere, Roland Pile comes right up to my face and pointed two dirty-looking fingers with nails like cock spurs right up to my chest and uttered in a hoarse and rattling shrieky voice, 'Hey, bway a long time now yu a fuck round mi yu know, yu tink sey mi a Buster B? Mi a come roun yu road Sunday mawning an if ah ebber si yu a gwine push mi knife way up to yu neck, yu hear bway?'

I looked down on him and said 'Hey, Roland Pile, move from out a mi face and go si dung and kratch yu batty pan tree thump bway.' Every one cheered and Roland Pile slumped away and sat on the culvert near Mass Alfie shop. The bus came and we left the square for school that eventful Friday morning, which I will always remember fondly.

MRS. D

Deep in the hills of North Central Clarendon in a district called Minho Wood, there lived an old lady by the name of Mrs. D. She was a Higgler woman who buys and sells farm produce such as citrus fruits, mangoes, bananas, plantains, and whatever produce was in season. She had a grandson called Benzie who was her right hand and was willing and able to do her bidding. She would take the Grey Mist bus to Coronation Market in Kingston every Thursday morning without failure. She was a much respected woman in her district and was known for her fairness and benevolence.

Benzie had a friend named Dread who impregnated his girlfriend. About a month later, it was rumored that Benzie's girlfriend Beverley was also pregnant. Benzie denied the accusations and refused to own up to his responsibilities. There was a sense of unease around Mrs. D house as she heard the rumor but said nothing to her grandson Benzie.

About three months after on a rainy Sunday afternoon, at about three-thirty, Mrs. D was seated on a rocking chair on her verandah looking out on a muddy footpath leading up to her house. You could hear the pitta-patter of the heavy raindrops pounding on the galvanized zinc roof. There was a bright flash of lightning and a loud peal of thunder echoing on the lush hillside surrounding her humble abode. She looked out in the distance and saw what appeared to be a young lady slowly approaching her verandah. When the figure was close to her outside step, she recognised the young woman and rose up from her seat and said, 'Beverly whey yu going inna blue boot and petticoat like yu going up eleven steps?' Beverly paused and said, 'Ah Benzie breede mi maam.' Mrs. D interjected quite calmly but authoritatively. 'Sey wha gal? Benzie breede you? Benzie can't breede woman, Benzie is a mirasmi baby, I take Benzie from him mother from him was three weeks old.

If Dread can breede a woman, Benzie can't breede woman. Soh if you nuh want mi and yu have anything yu betta teck yu foot outa Moses shoes before yu enta de mercy throne.'

Beverly started to cry. 'Look how mi did inna mi church and Benzie cum sweet mouth mi and breede mi and now nuh want fi own de baby. Mi ah go dung a riva go heng myself.'

Mrs. D blurted out, 'Gal nuh shed crocodile tears, 'cause de only way dat baby get anything is when him barn, and mi an Benzie must go up dere. Him foot must be long and him head must lang and pointed like fi Benzie. So if you no want mi and yu hab anything yu betta teck yu foot outa Moses shoes before yu enta de mercy throne.'

EXCITING DAYS IN ROCK RIVER

When I was at Rock River All Age School, I was the storyteller. When my friends had any information to pass on, it came to me first. It was then my task to disseminate this information to all and sundry, in whatever way I choose to do so.

My aunty operated a shop in Rock River Square, so I was privileged to be in the town on a daily basis. In fact I was involved in most of the activities that took place there. One economic activity that kept the town active was buying and selling. Many people would come from near and far to buy many products of trade. One major product was oranges. The Rock River Estate owned by the McPherson's, descendants of the white plantocracy who owned most of the arable land in the country, was the main supplier. On weekdays, it was common to see many people going to and fro with oranges on a variety of transportation of which the donkey was the most popular.

Many of these 'higglers', as they were called, would leave their produce in bags under the shop piazzas where they could be easily be loaded on the busses that ply the route to the towns of May Pen, Old Harbour, Spanish Town or Kingston. Star Liner Bus would travel on the Diamond, Simon, and Ginger Ridge to Kingston route. It would leave Rock River every morning at five-thirty to take the uphill climb. It could be heard from miles away in the stillness of the morning. The Grey Mist bus usually plies the Tanarchy, Moores, Chateau, May Pen, and Old Harbour Spanish Town to Kingston route. It usually leaves the square at about seven-thirty in the mornings. The Doreen's Transport Bus would come about eight-thirty. In those days, if you miss these busses you would have to wait for the Metro Bus that comes about twelve-thirty or take the odd private vehicles that travels to Chapelton, a district that was once the capital of Clarendon located on the main road to May Pen.

On weekends, Fridays, and Saturdays, Mr. Ottar would use his Leyland truck to transport people especially Higglers to May Pen, catering mostly to higglers from Mitchells' Hill.

It was a funny custom of ours to eat out some the oranges left by these people. A Morrison (aka Vwow) one of the regular orange buyers made these remarks, 'I tell Roland and I tell Randolph (two of his grandsons) to tie the orange bags dem properly so that those gluttonous boys dung ah Rock River can't eat out de oranges dem. They disobey my orders. Well, Roland is a big man now so I can't do him anything, but wait until my grandson Randolph come up here, a gwine slash him cross him face wid the double rope.' He continued to complain to his wife, 'Muriel when mi and Randolph go ova Busha Perkinson to pick the oranges so we can meck a living Randolph join wid him woman and man friend dem and start to stone mi wid oranges, me ha fi dodge behind the orange trees dem. Mi ungle hear pass me ears V—VA—VUP.

'If a wassan't cudden very site well Randolph would a lick me dung clean clean. And a tell yu Muriel, if it wassen't for me and Mass Tam; Busha Perkinson woulda lack him in a jail. Him foot wouldn't touch grung. Him would have to climb up eleven steps. Me have to sey, "Do Busha is me one grandson" (in those days police men were usually tall and muscular, and when they were apprehending males they would hold them in their belt and drape them up until they were tipping on their toes, hence, the expression 'Him foot wouldn't touch grung'.). (Climb up eleven steps refer to the Court House which were usually accessible by climbing up a flight of steps.) (It was a custom of children to throw oranges at each other as a form of sport. A Morrison thought that the children were throwing the oranges at him.)

TESTIMONY AT CHURCH

Jamaicans like to attend church services more than any other people in the world. It is a statistical fact that Jamaica is reputed to have the most churches per square mile than any other country in the world. The ordinary country people in the rural areas are even fonder of attending churches. It is a way of life for them; a place where they can meet, worship, gossip, and chat with each other as to who is wearing what, who is keeping which man, and so on. Church-going is a social and cultural activity that serves to occupy their time. The main church day is Sunday. They would have Sunday school for the children at about ten o'clock, then the service for the adults at about eleven. There would be night service later on and midweek service on a Wednesday too. The main religion is Christianity with a wide variety of denominations ranging from the more established churches like the Roman Catholic, the Anglican, Methodists, Moravians, Wesleyans, and Presbyterians to the Baptists, Church of God, Evangelicals, First Born, and Adventists, to the more traditional spiritualist churches like Poccomania and many others. There is also the Rastafarians who give credence to Emperor Haile Selassie I of Ethiopia as the Christ reincarnated.

It was a custom of these country people to give 'testimony' where they would affirm their faith in their God. Sometimes they would tell their home affairs or use the pulpit to tell off their neighbours. Mr. A Morrison is a typical example of this type.

One Sunday night, he went to church and when the time came for him to testify he said, 'Brethren in Christ and visiting friends, I greet you in the precious name of our soon coming king, Jesus Christ of Nazareth. Last night while I was in prayer, my grandson came behind me and started to draw me seed, all I could have done was to cut the prayer short to give ease to mi seed and fetch it a kick. If a couldn't give ease to mi seed there would be none, mi grandson would a draw it off clean, clean. That was not all, this mawning when a was getting ready to come to church and was about to put on mi suite mi grandson tied up mi trousers foot and mi jacket sleeve. I had was to untie them. Brethren, don't you think that de devil is testing my faith? Please pray for mi while I pray for myself in Jesus's name. Amen.'

FROZEN IN MY TRACKS

Early one Monday morning in the month of May, when the vegetation was still saturated with dew, I ventured into the precincts of the North Hall Road leading to the Rio Minho River. As I traversed the narrow winding path at a junction perpendicular to the train line, my optical receptacle focused on a headless apparition travelling towards me, suspended in mid-air. It was as tall as a JPS light post and as huge as the Ferry Police Station cotton tree. I froze in my tracks and felt cold sweat running down my back like a gushing spring. My tongue felt heavy and my head was swollen like an oversized breadfruit. Furthermore, my legs were shaking like a tree, yet they felt as if they were encased in lead. I was rooted to the spot, and believe it or not, it felt as if a boulder was on top of me. With outmost effort I tried desperately to extricate myself from the quagmire that was now engulfing me. Pushing and shoving but to no avail. I was trapped, trapped in my mind, body, and soul as if I was in a straightjacket used to restrain mad men.

Suddenly and without any apparent effort, I felt free and was now able to move my hands and feet. I lurched forward with rapid acceleration; not even Usain Bolt could match my strides as I moved like lightning. As I started to cruise on the crooked path, which was now turned into a straight, I felt an excruciating blow on my forehead and was jolted to a sudden stop. A huge protruding rock from the embankment seems to move in my pathway. My whole body was now numbed, and I immediately fell to the ground with a resounding thud. Instantaneously, I felt as if I was being lifted up by a powerful force that held me suspended in the air. In vain, I tried to fend off the intruder but found that my sudden movement caused immeasurable pain in my head as if it was going to explode. I opened my mouth to cry for help and realised that no sound could escape my lips as they were sealed with fright. I made one last attempt and to my astonishment heard my mother's soothing voice, 'All right, brother Jim, you are only dreaming.' I opened my eyes and surely I was dressed in my striped pyjamas that my mom had bought for me at May Pen market. It was such a relief to hear her reassuring voice and see that loving look in her eyes. I will never forget that dreadful night when I was frozen in my tracks.

GLOSSARY

Jah-meckyah	English	Jah-meckyah	English	Jah-meckyah	English	Jah-meckyah	English
grung	ground	den	then	drap	drop	orenge	orange
whey	where	pan	on	ratten	rotten	yu	you
kappa	copper	mek	make	sey	say	inna	into
yutes	youths	teck	take	sowa	sour	meds	meditation
praya	prayer	n'aan	eat	teck	take	wedda	whether
shuga	sugar	preffa	prefer	dawg	dog	fram	from
korna	corner	dat	that	n'aam	eat	lambs bread	kind of cannabis
ungle	only	nuh	don't	fi	for	skunk	kind of cannabis
unno	you all	badda	bother	trubble	trouble	barder	border
madda	mother	nebba	never	fia	fire	whey	where
fada	father	nutten	nothing	annada	another	trad	walk along
wuk	work	tun	turn	inna	in	ebbery	everything
de	the	dem	them	dis	this	Jam dung	Jamaica
wi	we	dere	there	fi	to	dawta	daughter
hab	have	heng	hang	meck	make	pickney	young child
cum	come	'yey'e	eye	wid	with	breede	impregnate
dung	down	clath	cloth	feget	forget	cudden	could not

Holland Bamboo	An arched bamboo grove in St Elizabeth
Fern Gully	A meandering evergreen area of lush vegetation in St Ann
Moore Town, Clarkes Town	Maroon settlements in Portland
Accompong Town	Maroon settlement in northern St Elizabeth
Bobbo Hill	Rastafarian communal settlement in Bull Bay
Pinnacle	First established Rastafarian community in Sligoville, St Catherine
Scotts Pass Nyiah Binghi Center	Rastafarian community on the border of Clarendon and Manchester
Pit Four Nyiah Binghi Center	Rastafarian congregational area in Montego Bay

Printed in Great Britain
by Amazon.co.uk, Ltd.,
Marston Gate.